Child Prostitution in Britain

Dilemmas and Practical Responses

Edited by David Barrett

The Children's Society
MAKING LIVES WORTH LIVING
A Voluntary Society Of The Church Of England
And The Church In Wales

First published in 1997

The Children's Society
Edward Rudolf House
Margery Street
London WC1X 0JL

A catalogue record of this book is
available from The British Library.

ISBN 1 899783 02 4

To protect identity, names of children,
young people and others have been
changed.

**The views of the contributors
are wholly their own and are
not necessarily the views of
The Children's Society.**

Contents

Contributors

Louise
Louise is now a student studying at college to be a community worker and hopes her experiences will help other people who become homeless etc. Louise also works part time at a bank to support herself while studying at college.

Paul Aitchison
Paul Aitchison was admitted as a solicitor in 1987. He is a member of the Law Society's Children Panel and the Solicitors Family Law Association. He set up his own practice, Aitchison Shaw, in May 1995. Aitchison Shaw is a specialist children and families practice.

David Barrett
David Barrett is Head of the Department of Professional Social Studies at the University of Luton. He comes from a social work background and has researched and written about children's and adult services in both the voluntary and statutory sectors. He has written widely on social welfare focusing most recently on child prostitution.

David Bowen
David Bowen originally trained as a teacher, but quickly moved into social work with children. He qualified as a social worker at Plymouth and worked in the west country and the Midlands. In 1986 he took a Masters Degree in Social Policy at Cranfield, looking at the education of children in care. He has been Dorset's Principal Education Welfare Officer since 1978 and is active in training matters for education welfare officers locally and nationally.

Richard Edgington

Richard Edgington is a Chief Inspector in the West Midlands Police Community Services Department. He has 29 years policing experience, including vice squad and related operations.

English Collective of Prostitutes

The English Collective of Prostitutes campaigns for the abolition of the prostitution laws which criminalise prostitute women, children and men, and for sex workers to be recognised as workers with legal and civil rights, including the right to police protection. The ECP monitors the effects of this criminalisation. It campaigns for viable economic alternatives to prostitution, safe houses and other resources for victims of violence of all ages, and provides legal and other support services to women, children and their families. Niki Adams, Claudine Carter, Susan Carter, Nina Lopez-Jones and Cari Mitchell, who have written the chapter, are active members of the ECP.

Jean Faugier

Jean Faugier is Regional Director of Nursing at the NHS Executive North West. She trained as a psychiatric nurse and later as a psychotherapist. Prior to her current appointment she was senior lecturer at the University of Manchester Community Nursing Professional Unit. She has undertaken a number of research projects investigating prostitution, HIV and drug misuse. The most recent of these was a study for the Department of Health about drug-using prostitutes and their risk behaviour.

Judith K Green

Judith Green currently works as a Health Promotion Officer for Sexual Health and Young People, and co-ordinates the 'Let's Talk About Sex' peer education project which trains young women to become effective sexual health peer educators in Leicestershire. In her previous post as youth work adviser at the National Youth Agency she researched and wrote *It's No Game* (1992). She has worked with Maggie O'Neill as a student on placement, researching the links between girls/young women in care and prostitution, and was also a member of the Nottingham Multi-Agency Forum on Prostitution. Judith is a qualified youth and community worker.

Cath Hayes

Cath Hayes works at the HIV/Sexual Health Unit in Rochdale; originally employed as an outreach worker in the unit, she is now primarily a trainer/counsellor. Previously, she was employed as Research Associate on a series of studies of HIV risk behaviour amongst drug users and between 1990 and 1992 on a Department of Health funded study of the health care needs of prostitute women in Manchester. She is actively involved in a number of voluntary sector projects working with young people and with prostitute women.

Sue Mulroy

Sue Mulroy currently heads an outreach project focusing on working with female sex workers funded by Health Promotion. The project offers a holistic approach to health and attempts to offer women information, support, advocacy and referral for client identified need. She has worked with Maggie O'Neill on identifying gaps in service provision with a view to facilitating multi-agency response to female sex workers. Sue has recently facilitated, co-organised and spoken at a Cheshire conference entitled 'Young People and Selling Sex' in order to raise awareness of the issues. She is a qualified youth and community worker.

Rachel O'Brien

Rachel O'Brien is Senior Press Officer for The Children's Society and co-author of *The Game's Up: Redefining Child Prostitution* published by The Children's Society (1995).

Maggie O'Neill

Maggie O'Neill is a Senior Lecturer in Sociology and Women's Studies at Staffordshire University. She has worked with women and young people involved in prostitution for the last six years. A founder member of the Nottingham Multi-Agency Forum on Prostitution she is committed to the development of multi-agency responses to prostitution which include the voices and experiences of women and young people themselves. Her preferred approach to research with marginalised groups is based upon principles of participatory action research. Key areas of concern are: violence against women and children; routes into prostitution from care; and policy-oriented practice.

John Pitts

John Pitts is Professor of Socio-Legal Studies at the University of Luton. He has worked as a teacher, a youth worker and an Intermediate Treatment development officer. He has acted as a consultant to workers in youth justice, residential work and agencies for the young homeless. He has undertaken research in the UK and mainland Europe into youth crime, youth justice and the social exclusion of young people. His publications include *The Politics of Juvenile Crime* (1988), *Working With Young Offenders* (1991), *Developing Services for Young People in Crisis* (1991), and *Positive Child Protection: A View from Abroad* (1995). His forthcoming book is entitled *Discipline and Solidarity: The New Politics of Juvenile Crime*, Macmillan (1997).

Mary Sargeant

Mary Sargeant originally trained as a documentary photographer. She recently completed an MA in Applied Social Research at the University of Manchester and is now a research assistant in the Nursing Directorate at the NHS Executive North West. Her research interests include mental health, women's issues, addictive behaviours and ethnographic research methods. She is currently looking at welfare issues in South Asia.

Ian Trafford

Ian Trafford has been a project worker with The Children's Society project, Safe in the City, for three years. Prior to this he worked with young people in a number of different projects in Manchester. He also spent a year working as a volunteer with Manchester Action on Street Health (MASH) which provides a variety of health-related services for men and women involved in prostitution.

Editorial Preface

Ian Sparks

This book has its origins in the work of The Children's Society in the early 1980s. Over fifteen years ago the Society met with statutory and voluntary agencies to try and identify the needs of young homeless people. All agreed that the area of need was vast, particularly for young people under 18 who had run away from home or local authority care. This consultation led directly to the creation in 1985 of Britain's first safe house, a Children's Society project for young people on the streets, and an expansion of this programme to other cities in 1986.

A planned programme of research followed, resulting in the publication of three important reports: *Young Runaways* (Newman, 1989), *Hidden Truths* (Rees, 1993) and *Running – the Risk* (Stein *et al.*, 1994). As early as the first of these reports highlighted the fact that young people on the streets were turning to prostitution to survive, an observation borne out both by the later research and by the direct experience of the Society's projects in Manchester, Leeds, Birmingham, Newport and Bournemouth.

To look in more detail at child prostitution, the Society commissioned a further piece of work, *The Game's Up* (Lee and O'Brien, 1995). And the figures this report contains of the number of children – boys as well as girls – being cautioned and convicted of prostitution and related offences make horrifying reading.

Encouraged by the constructive and positive response that we received to our Game's Up campaign from the Association of Chief Police Officers (ACPO) and the Association of Directors of Social Services (ADSS), we commissioned David Barrett to bring together under one cover the experiences and approaches of all the parties involved. In the chapters, the contributors share with us a wide and challenging range of views but, despite the differing perspectives, there is an encouraging convergence of opinion and a genuine aim to seek effective approaches to the problem.

Only two of the chapters reflect the work of The Children's Society: Chapter 1 by a young person, Louise, whose experience on the streets brought her into contact with the Society and Chapter 5 by our Safe in the City project in Manchester which discusses some of the dilemmas in practice. All other chapters express the views of the individuals or agencies that have written them. They do not always agree with each other – and The Children's Society does not always agree with them. However, the Society is convinced that by providing a forum for the sharing of all our working dilemmas and practical responses, there exists a greater chance for the development of workable solutions based on understanding and respect.

Chief Executive
The Children's Society

Foreword

Allan Levy QC

This valuable book provides an important forum for the discussion and analysis of why children are involved in prostitution and how we can respond practically to this dispiriting problem. Increasing media attention over the last two years has made the plight of the children known to many more people. Unfortunately, while the subject has produced increasing reactions of surprise, sympathy and outrage, in a practical sense not a great deal of progress has been made in providing remedies. Politicians and administrators in both central and local government have much to answer for. Prominent flaws which have been identified include a lack of co-ordination between various agencies and departments, and the absence of a national policy. We also seem to have been slow to take on board useful ideas coming out of Europe and elsewhere. The important messages in the UN Convention on the Rights of the Child, for instance, must not be ignored.

The application of the law in Britain has come in for particular criticism. Laws developed piecemeal and without any obvious unifying principles naturally in time are revealed as being complex and often inconsistent. Child prostitution is not, of course, the only area in which there is an obvious clash between laws available to be used to criminalise children and those which promote their welfare. An important theme of the book is that there needs to be a reconciliation in favour of welfare between the approach of the criminal law, and the Children Act 1989, and the Children (Scotland) Act 1995. It is vital that detailed reforming measures are prepared. General sentiments will not suffice.

Important recommendations covering many other areas are also made in this book. One can only hope for the children's sake that they will be acted upon.

Bedford Row, London
February 1997

Acknowledgements

Outlined below are some expressions of gratitude and a 'thank you' to the many who have helped in the production of this book.

When The Children's Society approached me to edit this book, it was flattering but also an excellent opportunity to contribute to its campaign regarding child prostitution – so thank you for the opportunity and the challenge. Encouragement and support followed from Professor Kate Robinson, Pro-Vice Chancellor – thank you Kate. Other friends and colleagues at the University of Luton have also helped considerably. Professor John Pitts (in addition to his chapter) and Professor David Berridge have given advice and feedback on so many aspects of the material. Lis Schild and Alan Marlow have also given me much moral support.

Graeme Brown, Helen Marsden, Mary Todd and Donna Reinhardt of The Children's Society Headquarters have all given me invaluable help – thank you all.

My own family, Gabrielle, Emma and Julie, have also helped me formulate ideas and proofread my material – thank you. The other contributors to the book have been patient and understanding about my editorial role. I have been very fortunate to be surrounded by such good support. I hope our efforts achieve the required impact.

The authors of Chapter 3 would like to thank Inspector Ron Holmes and Police Sergeant Brian Donegan of the Metropolitan Clubs and Vice Unit for their advice on the law relating to clients and pimps.

The authors of Chapter 6 would like to thank David Phillips, Youth Worker Development Advisor at the National Youth Agency and Maureen Whiskin for very helpful comments on the first draft of the chapter.

The Children's Society is grateful to the New Chasers Charitable Trust for its generous financial contribution towards this publication.

The Children's Society would like to thank the members of the Publications Advisory Group for their valued advice: Kathy Aubeelack; Ron Chopping (Chair); Sara Feilden; Nicola Grove; Virginia Johnstone; Karen Kirkwood; Dan Taverner OBE.

Introduction

David Barrett

Western culture is based on exclusion. Its society places 'others', women, black people, children, the old, those with alternative lifestyles, gay people, those with disabilities, as outsiders. A key element at the core of this domination and oppression is power and how it is exercised (Sibley, 1995).

Children themselves did not choose to enter the world or have a choice in their biological parents. Some say they are indebted to their parents for the gift of life. However, there has to be an enduring responsibility for the children we bring into the world and certain obligations have to be fulfilled. Some argue that, central to understanding these obligations, the notions of dependency and exploitation have to be understood (Dean, 1995). What is clear is that when children both enter and exist in the world they are vulnerable.

THE ORIGINS OF THIS BOOK

The Children's Society has been at the forefront of innovative work with children and young people who run away and end up on the streets. This work has its origins in research undertaken in 1981 into the needs of young homeless people in London which identified a glaring gap in provision for young people under 18 who had run away from home or local authority care. As a result, the UK's first refuge for children, the Central London Teenage Project, was opened in 1985. This programme of work has now spread to other areas in the UK and other agencies have learned much from The Children's Society's initiatives and practices.

Throughout the late 1980s and early 1990s a number of research projects concerning 'runaways', sponsored by The Children's Society (see below for full details), were beginning to establish with some certainty that a considerable number of young people who were involved in running away were embracing prostitution as a means of survival.

The purpose and outline

There can be little doubt that recent research has identified the connection between children and prostitution and, with sensitive publicity, the profile of the issue has been raised.

In the view of the contributors to this book, via direct practice and research, child prostitution is essentially the sexual abuse of children by adults who exert their power over children. We consider children to be up to the age of 18, as defined by the Children Act 1989 and the UN Convention on the Rights of the Child.

This book brings together a collection of chapters reflecting on the practice issues concerning child prostitution. The aim is to present, for the first time, a range of perspectives covering key professional groups and agencies who work in this area. The intention is to move forward the professional debate about how to respond to children involved in prostitution, preferably in ways other than through the criminal justice system. The book is therefore aimed at those at policy and managerial levels in a wide range of agencies who are concerned with children involved in, or at risk of involvement in, prostitution. Perhaps, most importantly, it will be both of interest and help to practitioners working at the practical cutting edge of this issue.

A broad approach is taken with the contributions and, remembering that the primary focus of the book is practice, no attempt has been made to resolve some of the ideological differences that are apparent between some of the contributions.

Contributors have been asked to convey their material from the perspective of their own specialism (but not necessarily an agency view) with the key consideration being that the piece moves forward professional practice in working with children involved in prostitution. Contributors have also been asked to consider the issues of gender, race, disability and sexuality as relevant.

Below a literature review is undertaken. It is not intended to be exhaustive but to inform the practice theme of the book. It does, however, demonstrate the growing interest in and problem of child prostitution, especially in the last few years.

The contributions

In line with the values and beliefs of The Children's Society we start with Louise, who recollects her own experiences of child prostitution. This chapter is not a comfortable read for those of us involved in protecting children. We must remember that this is a first person account, unlike some of the scenarios drawn up by other contributors to illustrate their chapters. Louise 'tells her story' and highlights the route she took into child prostitution as a vulnerable 13-year-old since suffering sexual abuse from the age of eight. She wanted someone to listen to her and to support her when she was most in need. Louise tells how her needs were repeatedly either ignored or not met. Many agencies were involved but with no single co-ordinated service response, Louise slipped into the sad world of the child sex industry. She tells her story most vividly.

The next two contributions examine the legislation and legal practice in relation to young people who are involved in prostitution. The first of these chapters gives an account of the wide range of Acts of Parliament available to the police surrounding the issue of prostitution. Edgington refers to the 'tangled' legislation and points out the numerous problems involved in enforcing such legislation. He also suggests that the legal response should be one of 'welfare' and not 'justice'.

Aitchison and O'Brien's chapter is divided broadly into two parts. The first considers the current criminalisation of children involved in prostitution and goes on to examine the criminal legislation as it relates to the adults who control or use young people for prostitution. The second part considers the Children Act 1989 and the duties it imposes on local authorities; it then discusses the legal representation of children in the context of civil proceedings. The authors show how the present legislation could be used more actively to benefit children involved in prostitution rather than punish them. They also argue that criminal legislation could be used more effectively to pursue the adult clients and those who control children in prostitution.

The next four chapters give ideas and insights from different agencies into how to work with young people involved in prostitution, including some of the problems encountered. The contributors also offer some practical responses.

The Children's Society's own work in Manchester is written about by one of its project workers and a consultant, Trafford and Hayes. They begin with a broad account of the project's work, focusing on the issue of young people on the streets and those involved in prostitution. They identify their practice policy and guidelines and state how these relate to a statutory framework and a partnership culture. The advantages and limitations of a streetwork model of practice, and the subsequent issues and dilemmas faced by children, workers and agencies, are also explored.

The chapter by Bowen, an Education Welfare Officer, argues that child prostitution is an issue for schools in cities, towns and rural communities across the country. Bowen suggests that schools can make a major contribution to the prevention of child prostitution through their acceptance and careful handling of child protection matters. He also suggests some creative curriculum initiatives and asks schools to provide a secure environment where children can make a fresh start from past traumas such as child prostitution.

The next chapter is written by three women with a range of experience in dealing with young people involved in prostitution from a youth work perspective. They outline their model of work and emphasise, like others, the need for a multi-agency approach in helping children at risk from involvement in prostitution. They strongly promote the use of the youth service as the pivotal agency that should be involved, yet emphasise the need to develop strong links with others, especially the health service, together with the need for policies and training to underpin the whole approach.

The contribution from Faugier and Sargeant looks at how health workers can intervene in the 'careers' of children and young people either involved in, or at risk of involvement in, prostitution. In describing some practical health care initiatives which have been set up to protect such children, the chapter also explores the associated issues of child abuse and neglect. These include poverty and homelessness, drug abuse, mental and physical health, and the role of health care professionals working within multi-disciplinary teams.

Following these professional perspectives comes the view from the street. The English Collective of Prostitutes (ECP) conceptualises some of the issues associated with child prostitution most radically (for example, rape, compensation). Other aspects that it comments upon, and its subsequent proposals, are similar to those of some other contributors (for example, decriminalisation, benefit changes). The ECP's campaigning style and politicisation of prostitution has often caused controversy. Here, particularly through its casework examples, the ECP offers many useful insights into the life experiences of young prostitutes, concluding with its agenda of 'what can be done.'

The last contributor, John Pitts, is well known for his sharp and critical analysis of matters relating to children and young people. Here his analysis provides a wealth of evidence that makes connections between poverty, sexual abuse and the involvement of children and young people in prostitution. He sees prostitution as a survival strategy and conceives of interventions which offer alternative modes of survival. However, he also suggests that new forms of professional practice and political organisation, at a local level (including us learning some lessons from abroad) could counter the pressures that drive children towards prostitution.

Finally, the conclusion offers a synthesis of the material in the book extracting the main points and identifying the most prominent themes from the contributors. There is an emphasis on practitioners' work with young people involved in prostitution and some recommendations are also put forward.

Before progressing further with what the above contributors have to tell us, let us explore what we know so far about child prostitution.

A LITERATURE REVIEW OF CHILD PROSTITUTION

This review of the literature concerning children and young people involved in prostitution follows the tradition of 'a coherent and carefully argued summary of what is publicly known about a topic' (Robinson, 1995). Helping professionals are spending more of their time with children who are accommodated because of sexual abuse, or who have had an involvement in the 'rent' scene or prostitution. Two major themes are the foci of the review. Firstly, the review of research offers several explanations for involvement in selling sex and particular attention is paid here to the role social policy has played, and its effects (Masterson, 1995). Secondly, and more recently with a health emphasis, some positive intervention strategies have been identified and explored. This approach does identify some cause for optimism for this group of oppressed young people, but it is often in the context of social policy militating against some useful initiatives. The review demonstrates a clear connection between government social policy and its effect on children's lives. The focus of this material tends to exclude child pornography, paedophile networks and ritual abuse. Although there are inevitably some overlaps and an interdependence with child prostitution, these areas have an increasing literature of their own (Kelly and Scott, 1993).

Child prostitution in the 1990s

During the summer of 1994, the media showed an interest in the plight of children working as prostitutes (Davies, 1994) and some of the debates on the subject, including issues such as homelessness and benefit changes. It is not just debates about prostitution that change – prostitution itself changes. It is relatively recently that the implied notion of prostitutes as women and girls has shifted to include men and boys (West and de Villiers, 1992; Foster, 1991).

One of the most recently adopted and widely used definitions when discussing child prostitution, to identify the nature of the behaviour concerned, is: 'the provision of sexual services in exchange for some form of payment, such as money, drink, drugs, other consumer goods or even a bed and a roof over one's head for a night' (Green, 1992). 'Child' refers to those under 18. Many researchers and field workers prefer the term 'sex worker' as it is both general and non-pejorative and acknowledges that prostitution can be seen as a form of work. This approach serves to link prostitutes politically with others in the sex industry, for example, off-street workers like masseurs and escorts, whose experiences will converge with those of 'prostitutes'. However, this term is most inappropriate in the context of children because of the inverse power relationships between adults and children, and it thus dismisses the exploitative nature of child prostitution.

The legal position regarding child prostitution is complex. A range of legal options are available from criminal proceedings to child protection. Children under 18 receive protection from the Children Act 1989. This may include those who are 'children in need' who are 'at risk' of 'significant harm'. Child protection procedures may be invoked and prevention may take place by 'accommodating' such children. Earlier legislation such as the Street Offences Act 1959, which sets the legal framework for loitering and soliciting, does not distinguish between adult and child prostitutes. This Act states that a woman cannot be prosecuted as a common prostitute unless she has been cautioned twice. However, it does mean in some cases that 15- and 16-year-olds have both cautions and conviction for prostitution (Marchant, 1993). Most of the literature is clear that interventions concerning children and young people involved in prostitution should be based on protection and not criminal procedures.

Who is involved?

Indicators of the prevalence of child prostitution are difficult to establish. Information tends to be fragmentary, being based primarily on voluntary agencies and localised research projects (Barrett, 1995). Although some practitioners who work with young people involved in prostitution will say that most are poor young white girls aged 15–16 with troubled backgrounds, used by middle-aged or older men, it is difficult to get a national picture to support such claims. National data about these young people is generally unavailable (Shaw *et al.*, 1996).

The wider view

The title of the Council of Europe's report *Sexual Exploitation, Pornography and Prostitution of, and trafficking in, Children and Young Persons* (Council of Europe, 1993) implies that child prostitution is connected with other major areas of crime. The report makes many recommendations to its member states, including the involvement of mobile units of social workers in specialist field work. As regards prevention, the report also suggests that particular attention should be paid to children in certain high-risk groups (for example, emotionally damaged children from broken homes, runaways, drug users and 'street children') who are easy prey for pimps or recruiting agents. It further suggests that there should be systematic and continuous control, by the police and social services, of places that are likely to attract young prostitutes and their clients (for example, stations, airports, seaports and so on). A subsequent follow-up research report was commissioned and published by the Council in 1994 (Council of Europe, 1994). The Netherlands is also a rich source of research material in the area of child prostitution (Barrett, 1994a).

Beyond Europe, the United Nations, via UNICEF, sees child prostitution as 'a universal phenomenon' (International Catholic Child Bureau, 1987). However, child prostitution continues to be big business in several countries that have ratified the 1989 UN Convention on the Rights of the Child, which expressly condemns sexual exploitation of minors, as did the subsequent 1992 UN Commission on Human Rights. However, during the summer of 1996, UNICEF, End Child Prostitution in Asian Tourism (ECPAT) and the NGO Group for the Convention on the Rights of the Child, held a World Congress against Commercial Sexual Exploitation of Children in Stockholm. A thousand delegates attended from across the world. The purpose of the Congress was to draw international attention to the problem of commercial sexual exploitation of children and to combat all forms of this exploitation in the specific contexts in which they occur.

The UK

In the UK, probably the most formatively theoretical work on child prostitution was undertaken by McMullen (1987) in the mid 1980s in Earl's Court. He wrote about young men and the rent scene and focused on the issue of power between adults and children. His influence still has a presence in that part of London (Gibson, 1995).

Health promotion issues have started to influence practice and research into child prostitution as the serious risk of contracting and spreading HIV infection has increased (Hanslope and Waite, 1994; Cockrell and Hoffman, 1989; Barnard *et al.*, 1990; Barrett and Beckett, 1996). In 1991 SAFE, an HIV prevention outreach project, identified young girls who had been prostitutes while in local authority care (Kinnell, 1991a). The girls reported that they had not been taught about safe sex. Jesson (1991) identified further connections between the local authority care system and young people involved in prostitution and highlighted the lack of proper preparation for young people leaving care (see also Jesson *et al.*, 1991). These Birmingham-based studies matched other findings (Biehal *et al.*, 1992). Jesson (1993) also identified the shortcomings of the social work response to young people and prostitution. A recent article gives an overview of feminist responses to adolescent female prostitution and the experience of young women in, or leaving, residential care (O'Neill *et al.*, 1995).

The relevance of running away

The importance of The Children's Society's work in 1981 has already been mentioned. However, in 1989 The Children's Society published a study of young people at Britain's first refuge for young runaways, the Central London Teenage Project in London (Newman, 1989). Key findings included a high incidence of abuse among those who run away and an over-representation of young people from residential care amongst those on the streets in London. The relationship between these factors has since received further attention and analysis (Ball *et al.*, 1991; Hendessi, 1992).

Following changes in benefits paid to young people and in payments to hostels, youth workers across Nottinghamshire noticed an increase in the numbers of young people selling sex to survive (Green, 1992). In the same year, Abrahams and Mungall (1992) studied the police Missing Persons Statistics for under 18s. They concluded that young people did not generally run away to the 'bright lights' but stayed in their local area. Again, there was an over-representation of young people from residential care amongst young people who were reported missing.

A study in Leeds (Rees, 1993) confirmed previous research findings that there was a high incidence of people running away from residential care, but also found that there was more running away from families than had previously been found. Indeed, running away usually started within the family, even amongst young people who later ran from substitute care.

In 1994, The Children's Society completed a further study of young runaways (Stein *et al.*, 1994). This revealed the experiences and survival strategies of young people on the streets who came into contact with four streetwork projects. The study found that the large majority who ran away did so before the age of 16 and one in seven of these young people had provided 'sex for money' as a survival strategy, a description the children and the research team preferred to 'prostitution'. The study also observed an apparently high incidence of cautioning and conviction of children under 18 for prostitution who, in other circumstances, might have been subject to child protection investigations under Section 47 of the Children Act 1989.

Arising from this, the Society carried out another study focusing specifically on the issue of child prostitution and the criminalisation of the young people involved (Lee and O'Brien, 1995). The report drew on the views of young people, the police, social services and voluntary organisations. It contains an analysis of Home Office figures relating to the cautioning and conviction of young people involved in prostitution and outlines possible future responses to tackle the problem effectively, including children being dealt with outside the criminal justice system.

Ways in and out of child prostitution

The link between runaways and their connection with prostitution is supported by further evidence from Europe (Van der Ploeg, 1989). The 'causes' of child prostitution, however, cannot be disentangled from factors such as poverty, family conflict, homelessness and abuse. 'Routes into prostitution happen within the context of complex lived relations' (O'Neill *et al.*, 1995). O'Neill's view is further supported by others (Kelly *et al.*, 1995 – note that this work has a particularly good bibliography).

Inadequate social policies also contribute to children entering, and militate against children leaving, prostitution. For example, gaps in the benefits system and shortcomings in adequate sex education both play their part. Clearly, there are several layers of discrimination – for example, homelessness, poverty, sexual orientation and ethnicity – which affect children who either are, or have been, prostitutes, as The Children's Society's Porth Project has shown (Patel, 1994).

Some intervention strategies

Few child care workers have experience of developing an understanding of the behaviour of young people involved in prostitution or of developing appropriate long-term interventions (Jesson, 1993). The problems for practitioners working with these young people are insufficiently recognised. Operating on the periphery of provision can mean that workers are isolated and do not experience the benefits of a multi-disciplinary approach that is necessary with child prostitution (Shaw and Butler, forthcoming).

Effecting change at both a policy and practice level is difficult (Pitts, 1991). There are, however, some grounds for optimism. In the Wirral, for example, young people themselves are responding well to a multi-disciplinary project where health and youth workers have successfully piloted a peer health education/safer sex project (Hanslope and Waite, 1994). This pilot scheme has involved outreach workers giving strong support to a group of ten young women who have themselves been involved in prostitution and are also drug users. The group in turn have been able to support each other and to share their awareness of health and related issues with other street workers.

Another recent study shows that social services departments must respond more quickly if they are to give preventive help and advice to young people involved in prostitution. Shaw *et al.* (1996) suggest a number of recommendations to assist service planners in developing an effective response to young people involved in, or at risk of being involved in, prostitution. In their comprehensive literature review on young people and prostitution they conclude that 'there is sufficient weight of evidence to require the offer of intervention by welfare agencies in the lives of young people involved in prostitution' and further identify key elements that might inform a productive, strategic service response, like the importance of a networking and multi-disciplinary approach (see also Barrett and Beckett, 1996).

Positive ways of responding to young people who are involved in prostitution, and which are less likely to alienate adolescents than some traditional social work approaches, include informal drop-in centres, advice lines and mobile services. Further methods and models exist both in this country and in Europe (Green, 1992; Jesson, 1993; Stein *et al.*, 1994; Barrett, 1994b).

Generally, however, such innovative service responses are either localised or operate via short-term initiatives which are mostly funded by children's charities. Few of these appear to have any long-term future and therefore any optimism must be treated with caution. Only a small handful of projects have some permanency about their funding; these too tend to be funded by children's charities.

A common plea expressed by young people in the sex industry is the desperate need for 'support' in coping with everyday problems. These can take many forms including difficulty in obtaining permanent housing and, similarly, difficulties in obtaining employment often after having experienced a disaffected and disrupted education.

Another recent report (Kirby, 1995) identifies yet another menu of recommendations based on research with young people on the street. There is nothing new identified and sadly, many aspects of the list are all too familiar, including homelessness, associations with care and a feeling of 'slipping through the net'.

We in this country could do worse than taking careful note of schemes in other European countries. Although many debates about welfare remain unresolved, some countries have identified the need for a 'lead' agency when dealing with the welfare of young people on the street. The Netherlands is one such country which has identified health as the lead agency in the field of the child sex industry. In this country, health, social services, charities, education and the police (and others too) all play their individual role and yet, lamentably, despite the best efforts of some, seem to lack effective co-ordination to deal with the problem of child prostitution.

But now we will turn to our contributors, who are from a wide variety of backgrounds and from whom we have much to learn.

1. Children Unheard: A Young Person's Experience

Louise

Until I was eight years old my world was normal. I got on with my family. When the abuse started happening at home I thought it was a general, normal thing that happened to everyone. The man who did it was part of my family. I thought it was love. At 13 I finally realised what had been happening to me and that it was wrong. I told my mum. I remember we sat in the kitchen and I told her and she said I was being silly. She didn't believe me.

My school teacher had noticed that there were bruises on me and that I was withdrawn. I told her what had been going on at home and she said I should tell someone else, so I did. But nobody believed me. Social services got involved. They asked me a load of questions. But what came out of it was that my family were always giving alibis so it was basically my word against his. Every time I talked about the times when we were alone together and when things had gone on my mum would say she was there.

Social services contacted the police. Talking to them wasn't very nice because of their attitude towards me. Right from the beginning I could tell they didn't believe me. I was an emotional wreck. My teacher helped me a lot though. I think the whole thing really pissed her off because she wanted something to happen but it was out of her hands. I think it upset her emotionally.

Mum threw me out because of what I had said. I was 13. She just asked me to leave and after that I never really stayed at home. The first night I stayed in the graveyard and I didn't sleep. I kept myself to myself on the street.

Soon my mum wanted me back home because she wanted the family and everything to be alright. My family are religious; they were very strong believers. I have challenged the person responsible but he still doesn't admit to it. He makes out I've got a psychological problem and they always believed him and I'll always be the black sheep of the family.

Mum used to call the police to come and fetch me. I used to tell them I didn't want to go home and that I wanted to stay out. The police knew I'd made a statement. They saw that I was emotionally upset and scared but still said that home was the best place for me. The police didn't pick me up every night because they couldn't find me, but when they did find me they'd take me home and then I'd run again. It was a regular occurrence. I forget how many times I ran away.

I stopped going to school because it was ten minutes from home. I was afraid that if I went, he would come to the school. He had threatened me with things if I told anybody about what had gone on. I used to be frightened of him.

I was fighting to get into care at 13. It wasn't just the issue of people not believing me. I wanted somewhere to stay and they were always trying to send me home. I wanted a safe place but nobody was listening to me at all. So I had to fend for myself and find places to stay. I had no money. At first I survived by stealing from shops and through help from friends. I never begged. After a while though, I lost most of my friends. I stopped thinking there was any point.

I started working in a massage parlour at 14. I saw an advertisement, rang up and went in. I started working there as a prostitute. They didn't exactly advertise that there were young girls there, but there were others about my age as well as older women. There was one younger girl than me; she was 13. Men would ring up and make an appointment. They'd come in for a massage and any extras. You had to pay the parlour for your shift but anything over that was yours. On a bad day you'd make £100, on a good day £200. It was £30 for hand relief, £35 strip and hand relief, £40 oral and more for full sex.

I would always protect myself. A lot of girls would say they do but don't because that is what most men want and some girls go unprotected so that the client will come back. I know a lad who used to be a rent boy who contracted HIV. He is 19 now.

A lot of the young people on the street are on crack and other drugs. They don't care about protecting themselves as long as they get their drugs. I never did, although I did test drugs out because I was surrounded by them. In the end, I thought I had enough problems; I didn't need a drug habit or a drink problem as well. You can start to rely on drugs or alcohol to blank things out but I always knew that the problems would still be there the next day. So what's the point?

I couldn't get accommodation. I did try to get a bedsit but I needed references. I couldn't claim benefits because I was too young. I didn't even try because I knew I wasn't entitled; my social worker had explained that to me. So I worked at the parlour for two or three days a week for a few months and then I walked out one day. I got sick of it.

I started working the street. There were other girls where I worked but I never saw any boys. Mostly boys work through nightclubs or other places. Where I worked a lot of the punters were businessmen. Most of them treat you OK. It has affected the way I feel about men. I used to fear men but now I don't. I see myself as better than them now.

Once I had a knife put to me by a punter. I got in his car and he said what he wanted and I did it. Then he pulled a knife on me and said he was going to stab me. I don't know why but I started laughing. He asked why I was laughing because he was going to put the knife in me. He was talking dirty to me. I got into that situation because I got in the car when I should not have done. We'd work in pairs taking it in turns and one girl would take down the registration number of the punter making sure he saw. The girl who watched out for me had gone with someone. I was supposed to wait but I didn't.

The police clocked me a few times and asked who I was. I would give them some bullshit story. But what was I doing out there at one o'clock in the morning? I used to lie about my age.

There were pimps that wanted to pimp me. They don't come straight out with it like: 'I want you to work for me'. They'd drive you round in their cars, they'd come up and start chatting away and ask you out. What they usually do is take you out and show you a good time, buy you loads of things. At that time, I thought I could have some protection but my friend told me not to use a pimp.

I saw other girls getting hit and one was murdered. Well, she disappeared as they say. She was 16. The violence is mostly from pimps. The police are not bothered, simple as that. With young people, like me for instance, they either choose to ignore it or take you in and book you and take your photograph. They never saw; they never did anything else. If they were in a bad mood they'd nick you. The clients, they never get any shit for it.

I was still sleeping out at different places and sometimes I'd hang around with people I'd started to get to know. It was like I blanked out for a while. I can turn myself off sometimes for a long period of time but after a while I can't and it begins to affect me. It's like being an actress.

You have to be an actress, you turn yourself off and you don't feel anything. When you are having sex with a punter it's just sex. No feelings or anything. I don't know what is in my head but I get it over and done with and get the money.

But I could only turn myself off for a limited period at a time and I'd have to leave and then go back. I started to get paranoid about the way I looked. I don't know why but that's when I knew it was affecting me. It feels like what I'm doing is going to show physically. I'd get into a depression and I'd get paranoid. It comes to a point when you just get so sick of men fucking you.

Apart from a drop-in centre for working women, I never came across any professional agencies when I was out working on the street. I wanted some help. I just wanted a home and I wanted to go back to school and try and get my life back to normal again. I thought, 'No one's listening to me'. Eventually I rang the Samaritans and they were really nice and they gave me information about The Children's Society.

I rang the refuge and I told the person I spoke to what had happened and she told me about how they worked. When I went to the refuge for the first time, I didn't trust them. I told them I wanted to go into care, that I wanted things to go back to the way they were, to go to school. They talked to me a lot.

The refuge contacted social services who sat in this room listening to professional people at the refuge who became like a second family to me, who knew the state I was in and who knew what they were going on about. But still social services were not prepared to accept what was being said. As far as they could see it then, and as far as they see it now, I should have gone back home because I had a perfectly normal life because my parents were religious and a religious family was the best place for me.

I went to a children's home but I didn't like it. There was a lot of bullying there. The staff were weird and they had no control. There were all kinds in there who needed help and support and the workers were supposed to give that. They used to sit in an office and chat about their own lives and that. They were getting paid for that. I was there for about two weeks. I spent time in three or four children's homes. At that time I needed help and support from the workers.

I talked to the staff at the refuge; I talked about the abuse and what had happened since. They gave me a lot of support, emotionally and otherwise. Basically, they believed me and it was a man who believed me and that was it. One day he sat down and had a chat. It had never happened to me before, the way he listened to me. You can tell when someone is listening to you and when they are not. Well I can.

A lot of professionals don't treat young people as equal. They think it is terribly sad but a lot of these young people are very streetwise. They see some jerk behind a table who has gone to college, to university and got a bit of experience in some children's home and thinks they know it all but they don't. You need people who are not patronising.

I was staying at the refuge for two weeks and then leaving when I had to go, and they would try and get me somewhere to move on to. But eventually there was nowhere for me to go because no one was prepared to put a care order on me. I was not considered at risk of significant harm. I was told that if I go home, I'd receive counselling and that is what they wanted me to do. I ended up at Christmas with nowhere to go.

There would be lots of case meetings where my mum would be there, social workers, the police and so on. Child prostitution and the risks involved were never discussed. They showed me the Children Act but social workers interpret it how they want. It is just guidelines and they'll interpret because they've got the power.

Emotionally I lived from day to day. I used to have a lot of nightmares and sometimes I used to break down. I wasn't aggressive. It was like I wasn't living in the real world; I was in my own world. I wasn't altogether there.

I went to see a psychiatrist which my social worker sorted out for me. This guy said to me, 'If you had three wishes where would you be?'. I just said I wouldn't be here for starters. He didn't know what to say. Most of his clients said they wanted money or Patrick Swayze or something. I have had counselling since. Sometimes it has helped but after a while I get bored with it. I have always dealt with things in my own way.

While I was going to the refuge, and for a while after, I didn't work the street. I went to college at 17. I wanted more money so I went back on the street to work. It is a hard pattern to break, particularly when you are young and there are no jobs for young people where you can earn that kind of money. There is also pressure on young people to have more things. A lot of young people are not prepared to live on the money you get from the social to pay for food and, for some, to provide for children. Also, there are a lot of young people who do the job and when they've done it they feel totally disgusted with themselves so they take drugs to block it out and get themselves into a vicious circle.

When I finished college for the day, I used to go down to the usual place and work. I went out with this lass who I am good friends with.

We'd go out several nights at 8.30 to 9.00. You'd get £200 on a good night.

I got cautioned one day. I remember this black guy came up to me and he said the police are out. I decided to quickly move myself around this corner but it was a back street. The van came round the back street and pulled me. I just said I was waiting for a friend and then they saw me again and pulled me again. They said they knew I was a working girl and knew who I was, and that they'd have to caution me. They were alright with me: 'What's a nice girl like you doing working', that kind of thing. Then they took me to the police station where I had my fingerprints taken and they went through my handbag. I had about 100 condoms in it which was quite embarrassing but they were really laid back about it. They dropped me back out where they found me. I've had no contact with the police since.

I knew that I was a priority for getting housing from the council. But I was never classed as homeless. They knew where I was but I was never on their computer. They didn't apologise. I waited for a flat and I am still waiting.

Social services put me in supported lodgings with this crazy woman. She got £80 a week. Her husband was in the nick for killing someone and she would take me to clubs with drugs and everything going round. You don't put a young person there. I also lived in a hostel for a while. I placed myself there. They are bizarre places. You can stay there until they find you proper accommodation. I was living in a room. I was there with another woman who'd fled violence. I was out of contact with social services and living off £36 a week.

When I was working as a prostitute I felt that what I was doing was wrong. It was wrong but I didn't have a choice. If there had been a choice there, if there had been someone there to have the power to do something, not just to wave a magic wand but to give me a little bit of security now and then and somewhere safe to stay, things would have been different.

I don't think for a lot of young people it is a choice. When I first started out, I had to do it. After a while, you get used to it. If someone had been there for me, if somebody had listened to me and helped me and supported me in my teens and given me the normal things a teenager should have, I may have been something else.

I can't take moralising. Prostitutes are looked upon as full of disease or full of drugs. You can argue up to a point that when you are 18 you can make a choice. But I've seen lots of girls, 13 and 14, working. They didn't see that they are vulnerable. They get into the pattern and they know at the end of the day they can always go back to it.

You just survive, or you'd just die, and I wanted to survive as I felt that I had to keep going because I wanted a better life. At that time, I just wanted to prove everyone wrong, that I wasn't a liar, and I wanted them to believe me about what I had said. When all that happened to me my life changed completely. I used to be this quiet vulnerable girl. I did.

2. Policing Under-age Prostitution: A Victim-based Approach

Richard Edgington

'Jacky' is 14 and lives with her boyfriend in a large Midlands town. She was in the care of the Social Services Department until she ran away from the children's home in the summer of 1995. Initially, she stayed with friends, sleeping on the floor or sofa. Sometime during the autumn she met 'Gary' who befriended her and offered her a permanent place to live. In Jacky's short and unsettled life, this was a stability she was unused to and she enjoyed the opportunity to have a home. Gary was kind, friendly and indeed appeared loving; although she didn't have any money, neither did she want for much. Gary managed to provide food, cigarettes and the few clothes she needed. In return, Jacky was expected to share his bed and have a sexual relationship with him. At first this was new, exciting and a demonstration of how much he cared for her.

By late autumn, Gary had started to grumble about the cost of keeping her and the fact that she could not provide any money for the upkeep of the home. At first, his suggestion that she could be 'friendly' to his friends and thereby pay her way was rejected by Jacky and he often became angry when the subject was discussed. The anger turned to violence and soon Jacky was sleeping with men Gary brought to the flat. In late November, Gary suggested that they go to London for a night out, an idea which immediately appealed to Jacky, and in early December they left the flat in mid-afternoon. At nine o'clock that night Jacky was caught soliciting for prostitution in King's Cross. Convinced by her that she was 18, she was told by police that she was going to be officially cautioned as a prostitute. Her details were recorded and she was warned that if she was caught and cautioned as a prostitute again, she would afterwards be prosecuted. One of the arresting officers suggested that she should seek some help in finding another job but didn't convince her that this was a real possibility.

Released from the police station after about half an hour, Jacky was quickly reunited with her boyfriend and they drove back home. Gary was angry that she had been caught and blamed her, but told her that money was very short and with Christmas coming up she would need to try again. The next night Jacky was driven into Birmingham and left on a dark, frightening street corner with few people about. However, she did attract customers and was able to give Gary some money. She was also given a free supply of contraceptives. For the next few nights, Gary drove her to Birmingham until she was caught by police but again convinced them she was 18. She was again cautioned as a prostitute and released. Despite using the same name as in London, there was no mention of that caution. After being caught in London and Birmingham, Jacky was driven to Leicester one or two nights each week. The rest of the time was spent with men brought to the flat or on the streets in Wolverhampton. After Christmas, Gary thought it was safe to try London again and for a few nights they were successful until eventually Jacky was caught and taken to the police station.

Her previous caution was known and discussed and this time she was unable to convince the officers that she was 18. Her real age was discovered and she was seen by a designated officer, a police inspector, and told that she was being taken into police protection as being likely to suffer 'significant harm' if released. After a while, Jacky was taken by a social worker to a children's home for the night. Jacky did not tell the police about Gary or that she had been arrested in Birmingham; her story about coming to London with a girlfriend was believed. The next day she was returned to the children's home in her home town and the day after that she ran away again.

Jacky and Gary do not exist but their story is typical of a young girl engaging in prostitution. Four out of the seven girls arrested in central London during the period from September 1995 to February 1996 came from outside London, three from the Midlands. The scenario also highlights some of the problems faced by police when dealing with prostitution, whether by adults or young people, boys or girls. Although prostitution is not illegal, prostitutes in the conduct of their business are careful and reticent about their work. Public condemnation of their lifestyle, as well as the unwelcome attention of police, tends to push it 'underground' and this exacerbates difficulty in identifying young people entering into prostitution. In some areas, older, more experienced prostitutes are credited with attempting to divert young women away from prostitution but this is more likely to occur where the population of prostitutes is settled and a new face immediately identified. Rarely would any attempt be made to report a new face to 'the authorities'.

The legislation dealing with prostitution is enshrined in four main Acts of Parliament: the Sexual Offences Act 1956 (offences concerned with the control and coercion of prostitution), the Street Offences Act 1959 (soliciting for prostitution in the street or public place), the Sexual Offences Act 1985 (kerb crawling) and the Sexual Offences Act 1967 which deals with male prostitution. These statutes have been enacted piecemeal in response to problems current at the time, without any over-all strategy or co-ordination. Some of the legislation is gender specific but the same offence is referred to: soliciting. The Street Offences Act 1959 applies only to women and the Sexual Offences Act 1985 applies only to the male customers of the female prostitutes. Female prostitutes can be arrested whereas currently their male customers cannot, discrimination which remains in force despite the 1967 Article 7 of the United Nations Declaration on the Elimination of Discrimination against Women. Sections 30 and 31 of the Sexual Offences Act 1985 relate to persons other than the prostitute gaining from her activities but each section is gender specific. Section 30 relates to a man living on immoral earnings and 31 makes it an offence for a woman, 'for the purposes of gain, to exercise control, direction or influence over a prostitute's movements.' The latter section seems to have been designed to remove 'madams' but the ultimate effect of both sections would appear to be to prevent women being coerced into prostitution. Section 32 of the same Act relates to importuning for immoral purposes by men – the male equivalent of female soliciting. The Sexual Offences Act 1967, whilst distinguishing between brothel keeping and living on immoral earnings, manages to make both offences applicable to both sexes.

Other, older legislation is also available to deal with circumstances which fall outside the remit of the Sexual Offences and Street Offences Acts. The Disorderly Houses Act 1751 has been used in prosecutions of owners of saunas or other premises where sado-masochistic or other unnatural services are provided. The Act could also be used for sexual performances which outrage public decency. Prior to the introduction of the Sexual Offences Act 1985, the Justice of the Peace Act 1361 was used to compel (bind over) kerb crawling offenders to be of good behaviour. This Act can still be used effectively where there may be circumstances not covered by the other more specific legislation. Other legislation is still occasionally used to deal with prostitutes acting in a disorderly manner and even public order legislation has been used successfully to prosecute kerb crawlers.

For organised and highly profitable activities connected with sex – obscene publications, for example – the Criminal Justice Act 1988 (as variously amended) is available to confiscate proceeds of criminal conduct.

Sections of other Acts of Parliament have been used to control prostitution, including the Town and Country Planning Act 1990 to close premises used for prostitution. None of the legislation specifically applies to young people but there are provisions in the Children Act 1989 which can be used if a child or young person comes to the attention of police as being engaged in prostitution.

Given the number and diversity of pieces of legislation, it could be expected that prostitution would be more controlled than many offences. The stance of successive governments since the 19th century has been to deal with the nuisance of prostitution and not the moral issues surrounding it – but the nuisance still persists. This, and the continuing necessity to use very old legislation, suggests that there is a requirement to revise existing legislation and at the same time make it more relevant to children and young people engaging in prostitution.

The scenario of Jacky and Gary can be seen in the context of this legislation. What will happen to Jacky as a result of the invocation of the Children Act? The officer discovering her age and identity has placed her in police protection under Section 46 because there is reasonable cause to believe that she would otherwise be likely to suffer significant harm. Under Sub-Section 1, the officer may:

(a) remove her to suitable accommodation and keep her there; or

(b) take such steps as are reasonable to ensure she is not removed from any hospital, or other place, in which she is then being accommodated.

To this end, the local authority has been informed so that it can provide accommodation and a designated officer has begun an enquiry into the circumstances as required under Sub-Section 3(e). The designated officer considers that by releasing her she is likely to suffer 'significant harm' and she has been accommodated by the social services department. All that is reasonable and allowable under the Children Act. But what would happen if her true age and identity had not been discovered?

The Street Offences Act 1959 creates the offence of 'being a common prostitute, soliciting for prostitution in a street or public place.' Apart from the demeaning nature of being described as a common prostitute, the process of being ascribed that description is problematic. The

Wolfenden Committee and subsequent Report which led to the 1959 Act was concerned with the danger of an innocent woman being arrested for prostitution. The Home Office Circular of Guidance for the Act (Home Office Circular 108/59) recommended as good practice the procedure in use in the Metropolitan Police District to safeguard innocent women through a process of cautioning. This required police to record the details of the offence, but not to prosecute, on two occasions. Once these two cautions were recorded, the woman became a common prostitute and any subsequent arrest would lead to a prosecution. Because such cautions are recorded locally, either within the police division, district or area or within the police force, a prostitute moving between areas or forces could be cautioned several times before becoming described as a common prostitute. This is difficult enough when dealing with adults but with a child or young person it only serves to prolong their dilemma for as long as they convince police they are over the age of 18 (after which the provisions of the Children Act no longer apply). For some, this may be a fairly easy task.

After conviction as a prostitute, details are recorded on a national computer database and are thus available to officers throughout England and Wales. Not surprisingly, this system can also be beaten if women use different names and details in the caution stage because fingerprints and photographs are not taken until arrested as a common prostitute. Younger prostitutes appear to do this more frequently. Whilst the cautioning system was designed to protect innocent women, it does little to protect younger people entering prostitution.

The other reason for the cautioning process is that it gives an opportunity for women to be diverted from prostitution by referral to a suitable agency. In the case of a young person or child this would, in the initial stage, be the social services department but the mechanism for referral would be by use of child protection procedures under the Children Act. This element of compulsion is one of the arguments against conditional cautioning for other offences (for example, burglary or theft). The feeling of many practitioners is that persons entering into a programme under compulsion and threat of sanction (for example, deferred sentence) if they don't comply, are less likely to be committed to the changes of lifestyle required by the programme.

In the opening scenario it was suggested to Jacky that she should 'get another job'. However well intentioned, this hardly constitutes an exit strategy and probably does not even meet the intentions of the guidance to use the cautioning process for that purpose. It is, however, about as

much as most police officers can give by way of assistance to leave prostitution. Often there is little knowledge by police officers of what exit
services are available, how contact can be made with them or which
people the service providers can assist. In addition, it is rather unrealistic to expect a person who has just been caught by the police and is probably confused and frightened, to take seriously advice given to them by
the person who interrupted their lifestyle.

Jacky, like many other young people entering into prostitution, was
already supposed to be in the care of her local authority but had in fact
run away. How successful will any intervention be, if applied by an
agency (for example, the local authority or other service provider) from
which she has already absconded? The problem facing police and social
services is how to achieve a timely intervention without being oppres-
sively coercive. Indeed, timeliness is important. Reported attitudes of
women engaged in prostitution are that for most, once they are involved
they can never leave or, if they do, soon return (Boyle, 1994). Even with
well-designed exit strategies and continuing support, there is considerable difficulty in breaking away from a lifestyle that is potentially lucrative or where there is extreme pressure from others to continue. For a
young person, perhaps experiencing for the first time an initial period of
stability without apparent restrictions or rules and the prospect of a continuing caring relationship, the opportunity or even the desire to seek an
alternative lifestyle will be remote. Given that there are few exit programmes available, it is unlikely that many young women will ever be in
a position to take advantage of them.

In the opening scenario Jacky was given a free supply of condoms.
Whilst most police officers appreciate the sensible harm minimisation
process involved, there is some concern that such programmes actually
encourage the continuance of prostitution. This is especially so when
young people are involved. There may well be some ignorance on the
part of police officers of all the services provided by some agencies and
they may see only some of the effects of the agency's activities, such as
the supply of condoms. There may be merit in some of those agencies
involving local police in the overall direction of their efforts. Whilst
appreciating that there is a question of confidentiality between the
agency and its clients, where under-age children are seen, a structured
referral to an exit strategy (for example, the local authority or a children's charity) may be helpful.

Given the negative effects of the cautioning process on younger prostitutes, there may be merit in reviewing this procedure and dealing with

young men and women coming to attention for prostitution in the way police would deal with a person of the same age who was a victim of sexual abuse. Police child protection units (in some areas these may be referred to as domestic violence units or family protection units) and their local social services departments have sophisticated arrangements for dealing jointly with child abuse victims. The advantage to police of treating young prostitutes as victims is that the joint investigation would assist enquiries into the circumstances surrounding the introduction to prostitution and may reveal evidence of any person compelling the prostitution who might, in addition, be an abuser. The medical examination normally undertaken of victims would not in such circumstances necessarily focus on evidence of sexual activity but may well provide evidence of assault which would tend to assist further the investigation of the pimp or procurer. In practice, the difficulties of identifying the age of the young person would still exist but may to some extent be diminished by recognition of the 'no blame' situation of a victim.

Such procedures need not necessarily ignore the fact that an offence has been committed but this could be dealt with in a way that does not involve criminalising the young person. In current Formal Caution programmes, especially those which provide an element of continuing support (often called 'caution plus' or 'caution with support'), there is recognition of the offending nature of the activity and programmes are designed to confront this in a non-punitive way. There would seem to be little reason why such approaches couldn't be taken with a young prostitute. To be timely, this type of non-criminal intervention should take place on the first occasion an apparent child or young person comes to police attention in circumstances involving prostitution. To take the Jacky scenario, the first occasion in London would have immediately led to referral as a victim, in this case to her home town's social services department, using the powers of Section 46 of the Children Act, merely to prevent a return to the streets and continuation of harm.

Another of the problems facing practical policing of prostitution stems from the secrecy which inevitably surrounds the activities. Estimates of the extent of prostitution are based on 'visible' activities, which may include off-street prostitution in one of the many commercial outlets from 'near beers' to saunas but cannot include those activities conducted in private homes. Indeed, these may never come to light. If the prostitute is careful and discreet, activities can take place indefinitely. In such an environment, a young girl can be kept and used without neighbours, friends, other prostitutes and least of all 'authorities' ever knowing about her existence. Her abuse can continue until she is no longer productive or a new source is found.

If the circumstances of her prostitution are discovered by police, what are they to do? In circumstances where an adult is involved, a period of observation may be necessary to gather evidence that prostitution is taking place, that someone, other than the prostitute, is living on the earnings of prostitution or that the premises are being used as a brothel. If the police know that the person believed to be engaged in prostitution is under the age of consent (16 years in the case of females with a male, 18 years for a male with a male), should they prolong the commission of the abuse and the offence by searching for evidence or should they step in and offer protection under the Children Act? If they adopt the latter course of action, the person living on the earnings, such as a brothel keeper or madam, is unlikely to be prosecuted for those offences and will remain free to continue their activities with another. If they seek evidence of those offences, they prolong the abuse and continue to leave a young person in danger. The usual response is to take action under the Children Act.

Prostitution is a market activity based on supply and demand. Until the Sexual Offences Act 1985, the emphasis was to control the supply side with little or no reference to the demand side. The 1985 Act was an attempt to redress the latter but, for practical policing, the measures in the Act are flawed. There are two sections: Section 1 is in two sub-sections and deals with men soliciting women for prostitution from or in the vicinity of motor vehicles; Section 2 deals with men on foot. Both offences require a degree of persistence but Section 1 adds an additional proviso: 'in such a manner or such circumstances as to cause annoyance to that woman (or any of the women) solicited, or nuisance to any other persons in the neighbourhood'.

The requirement to prove persistence is difficult if one considers the manner in which soliciting takes place. Men tour an area known to be frequented by prostitutes, identify the particular person they want, make an approach and are either accepted or immediately rebuffed. If rebuffed, it is most likely that the man will leave the area and if accepted, the transaction has been achieved and they leave together quickly. The experience of officers dealing with such offences is that men seldom make more than one approach and this is usually accepted. The Act does not define 'persistence' but certainly one approach is not. It might be possible to prove if it occurs repeatedly on different nights but this is not a recognised action. Another difficulty with this legislation is that whereas soliciting women may be arrested, soliciting men may not. Apart from the inherent discrimination in this, the deterrent effect is diminished since a summons can be issued which can be dealt with in the man's absence. A man arrested and charged with kerb crawling would appear in court and this is generally accepted to be a major deterrent to demand, given the wish to be as discreet as possible on the man's part. This particular demand reduction is only useful to street prostitution, which includes child prostitutes who operate from the street.

Within the sex industry, there is a feeling that working the streets is at the lower end of the market. New prostitutes often start on the street and seek advancement to off-street prostitution. Reducing street demand may make it less attractive for new prostitutes to make a start, especially those who enter as a matter of personal choice. The downside is that it may confine younger prostitutes to their places of residence where they may never come to attention and hence cannot be assisted out of the trade.

Proving nuisance to others in the neighbourhood is a more helpful approach, particularly as magistrates will be aware of the circumstances in their own area and cognisant of the complaints and general nuisance kerb crawling causes. They may therefore be more willing to accept evidence from a resident to the effect that there was nuisance caused and the evidence of the police that the particular defendant was part of that nuisance. Even using this branch of legislation, prosecutions are not excessive compared with the estimates of the proportion of kerb crawlers to prostitutes. Evidence quoted before the Parliamentary Group on Prostitution (1996) put an estimate that in Stoke Newington, kerb crawlers outnumbered prostitutes by between 5 and 10 to 1. Similar large excesses of demand over supply exist in most areas.

As a deterrent to kerb crawling, the average fine received is not particularly helpful. In a national survey of vice squads published in 1995, Benson and Matthews found that the average in 14 of the areas surveyed was £100 to £125. For many clients this does not represent a major inconvenience, especially when they may have paid £50 for the service in the first place. Certainly, when compared with the cost of a prosecution, currently around £300, and the policing resources involved, it is not a particularly cost-effective way of trying to reduce demand. Similarly, arresting and fining prostitutes, especially the younger ones, is not an effective deterrent and in most areas where police action is taken against prostitution, arrest rates of around eight prostitutes to one kerb crawler are average (Benson and Matthews, 1996); this suggests that prostitutes are not overly concerned about punitive measures.

Another difficulty in policing prostitution is the emphasis placed on it by police commanders. It is often not considered a priority, even in areas where it is prevalent, unless there are particularly vociferous public complaints about activity. Faced with demands from government, their own police authority and the public to address the 'harder' end of criminality, police commanders are reluctant to commit resources other than for limited periods (in response to a particular demand) or for a confined area. Although it is recognised that in areas where prostitution is particularly prevalent the possibility of other criminal activities is increased (drug taking, robbery of clients and prostitutes, assault of clients and prostitutes and all too frequently murder of prostitutes are associated with the areas most often used for street prostitution), the police response is at a very local level. There is little co-ordination within or between forces and little exchange of information.

Responsibility for policy is confused, lying somewhere between CID and Uniform with elements of child protection and community relations thrown in for good measure. At street level, prostitution is patchy and often confined to traditional and well-known areas which are quite resistant to change; it is understandable that without such areas commanders would be ill-disposed to commit resources to a force initiative outside their area of responsibility. At force level there should at least be a single co-ordinating activity which is cognisant of the changing environment and can disseminate good practice. Similarly, at national level there is little effective communication between officers engaged in policing prostitution, although in recent years a National Vice Conference has been successfully created, which annually provides a forum for ideas to be exchanged. These difficulties do not assist the deterrence or diversion of young people engaging in prostitution.

Generally, there is a concentration on female prostitution in most discussions on the subject. This is not because male prostitution is ignored by police, which it is not, but the male 'scene' is less noticeable and more often confined to off-street activity. Where the activities of men do come to the notice of police, either by complaints of male prostitution or the activities of male homosexuals not involving the exchange of money or goods, police reaction is likely to be an operational 'purge' on the area in the hope that this will be sufficient deterrent to prevent further complaint. There are some recent moves to negotiate with homosexual groups to diminish the impact of activity but this is sporadic and varies according to the local commander, rather than built into the operational structure of the police or other organisations.

The comments previously made about treating young female prostitutes as victims would not be out of place when considering young men. The same difficulties created by criminalisation of young people exist for young men as for young women. The same extended circle of criminality surrounds male prostitution and the same health dangers exist. If efforts can be made to remove young men from this environment by treating them as victims instead of criminals, the chances of long-term diversion from prostitution will be considerably greater.

The police response to off-street prostitution is again variable and often dependent upon the local commander's perception of the issue. Is it sufficiently problematic to be a policing priority? For many commanders the answer will be 'no'. Off-street prostitution is, by its nature, fairly discreet and unlikely to come to the attention of residents or authorities as nuisance, even where it is conducted in sex establishments, whether licensed or otherwise. This invisibility itself tends to diminish police interest. In addition, the difficulty of gathering evidence and the relatively low tariff punishment of offenders at court tend to make police operations against off-street prostitution even less cost effective. This does not help young people who may be forcibly engaged in these activities but evidence that there is widespread use of under-age young people in commercial establishments is not great. In some senses it is considered a 'promotion' to move from the street to premises and in most cases such a move is undertaken voluntarily.

Where there is evidence of under-age, unnatural or sado-masochistic sex taking place, police are more willing to intervene and will commit considerable resources to gather evidence. However, this must be tempered by the continuing harm that is allowed by this evidence gathering. Police powers of entry to protect people in danger are quite extensive and can involve the use of force. The Police and Criminal Evidence Act at Section 17(1)(e) gives police powers to enter and search premises to save life or prevent serious injury. Under the Children Act, an emergency protection order may authorise the applicant to enter premises specified in the order and search for the child with respect to whom the order is made. A court may issue a warrant authorising a constable to assist a person exercising powers under an emergency protection order to gain entry to premises using reasonable force if necessary (Section 48 (9)). With such powers, given sufficient evidence to suspect a young person is involved in prostitution in premises, police intervention can be swift and effective in removing that person from harm, especially if it is part of a joint investigation with social services or other agency.

Indeed, the most effective way of tackling issues of young people involved in prostitution is by joint effort between statutory and non-statutory organisations working in a co-ordinated way. Long and some-times painful experience has provided models of good co-operation in child abuse cases and the extension to young prostitutes is logical. In practice, there may be some difficulty convincing a 16- or 17-year-old engaged in a lucrative trade that they are in fact a victim, but a flexible and non-punitive approach stands more chance than a regular court appearance and a £20 fine.

In summation, the difficulties for police in dealing with prostitution are compounded by the fact that the person(s) concerned may be under age and in some danger. The legislation is tangled and in most cases not very effective in achieving the desired ends. The cautioning process, in turning a woman into a prostitute, hinders rather than helps her escape from the lifestyle, and the cyclical and punitive nature of prosecution does not act as a deterrent.

An imaginative revision of the legislation making it universally applica-ble and easier in practice to enforce is required. Such revised legislation should also make separate provision for children and young people engaging in prostitution, in particular making exit from the lifestyle more structured and not reliant on words of advice from arresting offi-cers. The addition of a power of arrest to the offence of kerb crawling and removal of the requirement for persistence and annoyance/nuisance may make that legislation more effective as a deterrent. Imposition of stiffer penalties for people convicted of off-street prostitution offences, living on immoral earnings or brothel keeping may make police action more cost-effective and therefore more attractive to police commanders.

The cautioning process designed to prevent innocent women being arrested as prostitutes and to help divert others from that lifestyle has a counterproductive action when dealing with young people. It is not part of legislation but was given as good practice in 1959; its usefulness even to protect older but innocent women must be questionable nearly 40 years later. Very young (under-age) people engaging in prostitution would be better served and protected if they were treated as victims of sexual abuse rather than offenders. For those between 16 and 18, a flexi-ble but non-punitive approach could be adopted. This could involve a similar type of approach to the 'caution with support' programmes employed for other offences by youth justice departments throughout the country. This need not avoid confronting the person with the fact that their actions were illegal but falls short of criminalisation and stigmatisation as a common prostitute. For young people over the age of 18 arrested for prostitution, it would be helpful if a structured referral programme could be arranged prior to their release from the police station. For those more resistant to such strategies, a way of breaking the Street–Arrest–Court–Fine–Street cycle needs to be achieved. Imprisonment for non-payment of fines is not an effective deterrent and many prostitutes regard it as a blessed relief rather than a punishment, especially where a violent pimp is involved.

In most areas of police action against criminality and offending there is an understanding that partnership and co-operation between agencies offers immediate benefits. Whilst there have been some cases of multi-agency projects, for example, Lumb Lane in Bradford and Operation Welling around King's Cross in London, partnerships against prostitution are not as prolific as they are with other types of offending. With the association of numerous other types of offending behaviour with prostitution, it might be thought that to reduce one would reduce the others. Perhaps it is because the impact of prostitution is confined to very small areas that, by and large, the impact on the majority of citizens is small, and perhaps because more people actually seek the services than offer them, there isn't such necessity to intervene. Where multi-agency work has been tried it does appear to have been successful in assisting women to leave the profession. Multi-agency co-operation has been successful in harm minimisation in drug use and there may well be opportunity for similar co-operation in prostitution. Even if such co-operation was limited to a profile-raising exercise so that each agency knew of the others' existence, aims and objectives, and had some mechanism for referring clients to each other, this would be a step forward. It would assist officers in trying to divert people from prostitution.

It would be encouraging to think that Jacky managed to escape from prostitution but it is unlikely that she would do so. Even with 'no blame' strategies there are strong incentives to remain: it can be lucrative, hours are flexible and at the top of the market there is a certain glamour that is almost socially acceptable. Unfortunately, many do not graduate beyond the streets, money is taken from them by their pimps, their health is damaged by drug and alcohol abuse and by disease. They are preyed on by criminals and their clients, castigated by neighbours and residents and very often let down by procedures designed to help them. If just one Jacky can be helped to escape this lifestyle, it must be worthwhile trying.

3. Redressing the Balance: The Legal Context of Child Prostitution

Paul Aitchison and Rachel O'Brien

This chapter has been written with a view to providing a general overview of the way criminal and civil legislation relates to children involved in prostitution. In addition, the authors have attempted to show how the present legislation could be used more actively to benefit children involved in prostitution rather than to punish them. Children exploited in the sex industry are caught between two possible responses from society – either one of punishment or one of protection. It is the authors' view that the more appropriate response is to rely on inter-agency co-operation to protect children from the harm they suffer as a result of their involvement in the sex industry. At present, such protection as can be afforded to children who find themselves in these circumstances is done so by virtue of the Children Act 1989 and the guidance issued by the Home Office in connection with this statute.

The chapter is divided into four sections. Rachel O'Brien, in the first section, summarises how the criminal law relates to, and is currently being used against, children and young people involved in prostitution. She goes on in the second section to suggest some ways in which criminal legislation could be used more actively to pursue the adult clients of, and those who control, children involved in prostitution. The third section, by Paul Aitchison, outlines the framework provided by the Children Act 1989 for the protection of children. He concludes in the fourth section by discussing some of the practice issues for solicitors of advising and representing children in the context of related civil legal proceedings.

THE CURRENT SITUATION

Section 50 of the Children and Young Persons Act 1933 provides that no one under the age of ten can be guilty of an offence, although the United

Nations Committee on the Rights of the Child, publishing its assessment in 1995 of the progress of the British government in implementing the UN Convention on the Rights of the Child, recommended that the age of responsibility be raised. From the age of ten up to his or her fourteenth birthday, a child can only be charged with a criminal offence if the prosecution can prove that the child knew that what s/he was doing was wrong. At the age of 14 a child is deemed to have full responsibility for his or her actions. As legislation relating to soliciting and loitering makes no age distinction, it is possible for children as young as ten to be charged for offences relating to prostitution.

Home Office figures show that there has been a significant number of cautions and convictions relating to children under 18 involved in prostitution. Between 1989 and 1995 a total of 2380 cautions were issued and 1730 convictions were secured against those under 18 in England and Wales (see Appendix 1). Although during this period there was an overall reduction in the numbers relating to young people aged 17, there was a 40% rise in those relating to children aged 16 and under between 1989 and 1994. However, 1995 figures show a similar number of cautions and convictions of under 17-year-olds as was the case in 1989. These figures include a caution issued against a 10-year-old, 52 convictions secured against girls under 16 and 52 convictions against boys under 18 (*Source:* Home Office). This is despite the fact that girls under the age or 16 cannot in law consent to sexual intercourse and boys under 18 cannot in law consent to homosexual sex. This contradiction exists partly because it is not prostitution itself that is illegal but soliciting, loitering, living off immoral earnings and other related offences. So the offences that children and young people find themselves facing relate not to sexual activity *per se* but to their conduct in a public place.

The vast majority of the above cautions and convictions were made under the Street Offences Act 1959. The Sexual Offences Act 1956 was cited against young males. Home Office figures also suggest that some young people on the street have been charged with aiding and abetting kerb crawling under the Sexual Offences Act 1985 (Lee and O'Brien, 1995).

The Street Offences Act 1959 set much of the legal framework for dealing with loitering and soliciting. Under Section 1 of the Act it is an offence for 'a common prostitute to loiter or solicit in a street or public place for the purposes of prostitution'. Guidelines issued on the Act advise police to issue two warnings or 'street cautions' before making an arrest. While police and courts have used Section 1 of the 1959 Act against males, a high court ruling in 1994 concluded that a common prostitute can only be female (*DPP* v. *Bull* [1994] 4 All ER 411).

The legal position for boys and young men involved in prostitution is different and overlaps with legislation relating to buggery. In addition to being charged under the Sexual Offences Act 1956, young males are also likely to be charged with offences such as obstructing the highway. As a result, official statistics do not give a clear indication of how many boys are charged with offences relating to prostitution.

Under Section 12 of the Sexual Offences Act 1956 it is an offence for a person to commit buggery with another person unless both parties are over 18, and consent, and the act takes place in private. Young men involved in prostitution could be charged with this offence but so could young men involved in consensual activity where no money or goods are exchanged. Under Section 32 of the 1956 Act it is an offence for a man to persistently solicit or importune in a public place for immoral purposes. Like the Street Offences Act 1959, the 1956 Act makes no distinction between a child and an adult. However, there is no requirement under Section 32 of the 1959 Act for two 'street cautions' to be issued before making an arrest for soliciting. Whereas the Criminal Justice Act 1982 replaced imprisonment for offences under Section 1 of the Street Offences Act 1959 with a fine, the maximum penalty for soliciting or importuning under the Sexual Offences Act 1956 is two years.

Once a male or female under the age of 18 has been arrested there are a number of stages at which criminal proceedings could be dropped, a caution recommended or a welfare-led response taken (the child could receive a combination of these responses). One such stage could be at referral to the local juvenile liaison panel. If a decision is made to charge a young person, papers will be sent to the Crown Prosecution Service (CPS). The CPS is bound by the Code for Crown Prosecutors in accordance with Section 10 of the Prosecution of Offences Act 1985. The Code has two central principles: that prosecution would be in the public interest – this includes taking into account the distress to the victim of the offence – and that there is sufficient evidence to proceed. The Code highlights the need to take into account the 'irreparable harm' that a conviction can have on the future prospects of a young person. The CPS stresses that prosecution should always be regarded as a serious step and that, wherever possible, the objective should be to divert juveniles from court.

If it is decided that a child or young person will be prosecuted, s/he must appear before a youth court at the earliest possible date. Young people under the age of 18 can be detained in custody while on remand waiting for a court date. Magistrates have available to them a range of choices once a young person charged with an offence relating to prostitution appears before them. In addition to fines, and custodial sentences in the case of boys, a magistrate can choose to hand down an absolute or conditional discharge, place a young person on a supervision order or hand down a combined sentence. In practice, many young people charged with soliciting-related offences are punished through the use of fines. It has been pointed out by others that, given the situations these children and young people are in, often the only way to pay fines is to return to the street.

THE LAW AND ADULT PERPETRATORS

Attempts to redefine the children involved in prostitution as victims of abuse leads to a similar rethinking of the adult offenders involved. This has led to an increasing awareness that new responses – cultural, practical and legal – are needed to deal with the adult offenders. Very generally, this entails redefining adult involvement in child prostitution more accurately as child sexual abuse.

Practically, this has meant an increasing recognition that children involved in prostitution should be dealt with by police juvenile protection teams rather than vice squads, whose most common strategy for dealing with prostitution has been the arrest of those soliciting (Benson and Matthews, 1995). It has also led to a review by the Association of Chief Police Officers of the emphasis placed on protecting children and the pursuit of adult offenders announced in a joint statement by the Association of Chief Police Officers, the Association of Directors of Social Services and The Children's Society in August, 1996. This highlights the need for police officers who are dealing with prostitution to be aware of their duties under the Children Act to protect children and young people.

Outlined below is the current legal framework as regards clients and pimps, and other relevant legislation which could be used by the police, the CPS and courts when dealing with adults having, or attempting to have, sexual activity with children and young people, and those profiting from that abuse. Some of what is suggested will rely heavily on increased resources and an emphasis on the investigation of offenders for cases to be accepted first by the CPS and for successful convictions to be secured. This is particularly significant given that children and young people are not always willing to testify and so other evidence such as surveillance could be crucial. This should be consistent with the emphasis placed on more traditional child protection procedures and investigations which necessitate close inter-agency co-operation in working with children on disclosure, providing witness protection and post-disclosure support.

The authors recognise that the pursuit of adult offenders is highly complex and is not a solution in itself. However, a more effective cultural and practical response to child prostitution requires better use of existing legislation, on the one hand, for working with children and young people in order, on the other hand, to deter adults from using children and young people in this way.

Clients

Some agencies working with young people have reported incidents of men openly seeking out children on the street for sex. Likewise, the Home Office figures cited above show that there are some very young children involved. Wherever there are children on the streets or in flats selling sex, there are 'customers' who use them. However, relatively few adult offenders are ever convicted for kerb crawling and certainly not for offences relating to the abuse of children (Holmes, 1995).

This is in part because the men who pay for sex with children and young people have not generally been viewed – by themselves or others – as child sex offenders in the same way as they would be if they were to abuse within either a family or a work context.

Kerb crawling

Under Section 1 of the Sexual Offences Act 1985, a man commits an offence if he solicits a woman for the purposes of prostitution if he is either in, or has just got out of, a vehicle and if he is persistent. This section also provides for a man being guilty of an offence if his behaviour causes, or is likely to cause, a nuisance to women or others in the neighbourhood.

It is also an offence under Section 2 of the Act to persistently solicit by foot a woman or women for the purpose of prostitution. These are non-arrestable offences and are punishable with a maximum fine of £1000 (level 3 on the standard scale), although the average fine imposed is often significantly less (Holmes, 1995).

The police have argued that it is hard to gather enough evidence to prove persistence and have suggested this word be removed from the legislation (Benson and Matthews, 1996). However, recent case law has suggested that the degree of repetition necessary for a man to commit an offence under Section 1 of the 1985 Act is slight and that two invitations appear to be sufficient. In 1994 there were 7029 convictions against females – and some children – for soliciting under the Street Offences Act 1959 and only 1158 secured for kerb crawling. It has been proposed that giving police powers of arrest would help redress this balance. To be charged, the client must have indicated that he is seeking the services of a prostitute either verbally or by some other action such as sounding a car horn. The Act makes no distinction regarding the age of the person solicited for services.

It is fundamentally inappropriate for adults who are seeking out children for sex to be dealt with as kerb crawlers or as a nuisance as a matter of course. If men are to be deterred from seeking sex with children, there needs to be an awareness that they face far higher penalties which have very different implications for themselves and, possibly, their own families.

It may be possible for the police and CPS to use Section 1 of the Indecency with Children Act 1960, which prohibits an act of gross indecency with or towards a child under 14 or incitement of a child under that age to an act. If police can gather evidence that an adult suggested an act of gross indecency, they do not have to prove that adult touched the child to secure a conviction. A passive response from the child is not a defence and the maximum penalty is two years imprisonment. Third party eye witness testimony could be sought in cases such as these.

Sexual intercourse and assault

Under Section 5 of the Sexual Offences Act 1956 it is an offence for a man to have sexual intercourse with a girl under the age of 13. The consent of the victim is no defence and the maximum penalty is life imprisonment. Attempting to commit this offence carries a maximum penalty of seven years imprisonment.

Section 6 of the Act provides for a similar offence for sexual intercourse with a girl under 16 and carries a maximum penalty of two years imprisonment. The only statutory defences here are if the man is under the age of 24, has not been charged with a previous like offence and believes, and has reasonable cause to believe, she is over 16. Under Section 15, it is an offence for a man to make an indecent assault on a male. If the boy is under 16 years of age there is no defence of consent. The maximum penalty is ten years imprisonment.

It is an offence under Section 14 for a man to make an indecent assault on a woman. As a girl under 16 cannot legally consent to sex, any sexual activity with a girl under 16, whether with her consent or not, is sexual assault. The maximum penalty is ten years imprisonment. The legislation makes no distinction between consensual sex between two males under the age of 18 and a situation where an adult has solicited sex from a boy or young man.

The 1956 Act cannot be used to secure convictions against men having consensual sex with 16- and 17-year-old girls. The Children Act 1989 does, however, impose on police a duty to protect any person under the age of 18 who is at risk of significant harm.

To secure a conviction, the police are likely to need either to catch the man having sexual intercourse, or assaulting the young person, or to have physical evidence to prove sexual intercourse has taken place. In cases such as this, it may be essential to gain the co-operation of the victim in agreeing to appear in court and to undergo physical examination. Clearly, if the police believe that an adult they have under surveillance is about to sexually assault a child, they have to take action before the act takes place.

The above legislation is probably the most likely to act as a deterrent to adult offenders because, if convicted, the penalties are higher and the offender would have a sexual offence on his record. With enhanced inter-agency co-operation and more emphasis on information and evidence gathering, the police would have a stronger chance of persuading the CPS to take a case against an adult offender for having or attempting to have sexual intercourse with a child.

Greater surveillance and information sharing could also be used to gather evidence against a man who solicits a girl under 16 or a boy under 18. This is likely to rely heavily on the co-operation of the child or young person. If the child is under 14, an option could be to use Section 1 of the Indecency with Children Act 1960 relating to gross indecency. Not knowing the age of the child would be no defence. It may also be possible for the police and CPS to use the offence of outraging public decency. This is a common law offence as set down in *Knuller (Publishing, Printing and Promotions) Limited* v. *DPP* [1973] AC 435 continued in *Gibson* [1990] 2 QB 619.

If a client is violent or threatens violence towards a child or young person, other legislation may be employed such as the Criminal Justice Acts or sections of the Offences Against the Person Act 1861 relating to actual or grievous bodily harm.

Pimps

It is not known how many children and young people involved in prostitution are controlled or recruited by pimps. This is in part due to the low visible profile pimps will have in contrast to young people soliciting. In addition, many of those children and young people being controlled by an adult will not identify that adult as a pimp but as a friend or boyfriend (Lee and O'Brien, 1995; Barnardo's, 1996). This reflects the level of fear and control that pimps can engender.

The experience of the police and other agencies suggests that the role of adults in the recruitment and control of young people is significant and a growing problem. Although police authorities are in some areas attempting to clamp down on pimps, the selling of sex with children in return for money is still a relatively low-risk way of obtaining financial – and often sexual – rewards for the adults involved.

Living off immoral earnings

Under Section 30 of the Sexual Offences Act 1956, it is an offence for a man knowingly to live wholly or in part on the earnings of a prostitute. This can include a man who lives with a woman involved in prostitution, is habitually in the company of a prostitute or who exercises control, direction or influence over a prostitute's movements in a way that shows he is aiding, abetting or compelling her prostitution with others.

Section 31 of the Act applies to women living off the immoral earnings of female prostitutes and is in practice more likely to be used by the police and courts against those running establishments such as massage parlours and escort agencies where prostitution takes place. Section 5 of the Sexual Offences Act 1967 has a similar offence as regards living off the immoral earnings of male prostitution and requires similar evidence.

Charges for all of the above can only be brought when it is established that there is a prostitute involved. In court, the burden of proof rests on the defence if, and only if, the prosecution has satisfied the court that the woman he lives or habitually consorts with is a prostitute.

The Acts make no specific provision for the involvement of juveniles. If adults who are controlling children and young people are to be charged with living off immoral earnings, there is a need for the child or young person to be, or have already been, labelled a prostitute. This may be determined by any record of them having been cautioned and/or convicted for soliciting or related offences and conflicts with emphasising that children and young people involved in prostitution are victims of exploitation and abuse.

Procuration

Under Section 2 of the Sexual Offences Act 1956, it is an offence to procure a female by threats or intimidation to have unlawful sexual intercourse in any part of the world. Under Section 23, there is a specific offence for procuring females under the age of 21. The maximum penalty is also two years. It is also an offence under Section 3 for a man to use false pretences and under Section 4 to apply, administer or cause to be taken any drug or matter with intent to stupefy or overpower a woman with the aim of enabling any man to have unlawful sexual intercourse with her. A person cannot be convicted of offences under the above sections with the evidence of one witness unless the witness's evidence is corroborated by other evidence. Under Section 22, it is an offence to procure a woman to become a common prostitute. The maximum penalty is two years imprisonment.

Section 24 of the Police and Criminal Evidence Act 1984 provides for powers of summary arrest and these are applicable to offences under Section 22 and 23 of the Sexual Offences Act 1956. The charge of procurement is dependent on the female 'becoming' a prostitute and therefore successful prosecution is unlikely where a child or young person has already been cautioned and/or convicted for soliciting.

Section 19 of the Act makes it an offence to take a girl under the age of 18 out of the possession of her parent or legal guardian against her/his consent for the purposes of having unlawful sex with a man or men. Section 20 provides for a similar offence relating to girls under 16. The maximum penalty for both offences is two years imprisonment. A man committing a similar offence against a woman under Section 17 of the Act could face 14 years imprisonment.

Under Section 28 of the Act, it is an offence for a person to cause or encourage the prostitution of, intercourse with or indecent assault on a girl under 16. Under this section, the emphasis is not on 'becoming' a prostitute and applies to allowing continued involvement. The person in question is defined as someone who is responsible for the girl. This includes: either her parent or legal guardian; someone who has 'actual possession or control' of her or to whose charge she has been committed; or any other person who has custody, charge or care of her. If this section is used against an adult offender in relation to a child under 13, the highest penalty he could receive is two years imprisonment.

While it is possible that in some cases the adults procuring a child or young person may be legally responsible for them, this is not usually the case. If there is enough evidence to prove that a pimp has 'actual possession or control' of a child under 16, then it may be possible to bring a conviction under this section. Police and voluntary agencies working with children on the streets have found that some children they worked with had become completely under the control of their pimps to the extent that they were 'willing victims', even when suffering extreme violence and degradation (Barnardo's, 1996).

Under Section 4 of the Sexual Offences Act 1967, it is an offence for a man to procure another male, but there is no age discrimination. If a child or young person under the age of 18 is involved, the prosecution may use Section 15 of the Sexual Offences Act 1956 relating to unlawful sexual intercourse.

Securing convictions for procuring is difficult. In court, the prosecution may need to prove intent to procure a female for work in a brothel and for actual sexual intercourse with a third party, rather than other sexual activity. However, under Section 22 of the 1956 Act, lewdness is the basis element of the offence and not actual sexual intercourse. The suggestion of sexual activity could be enough to warrant arrest. Corroborating evidence is needed to secure a conviction under Section 22 and 23 of the 1956 Act.

Particularly where a young person is over 16, a successful conviction is likely then to depend on the child or young person having no previous cautions or convictions for soliciting and may mean proving that the pimp intended her to have actual sexual intercourse. In 1994, there were only 92 convictions against men and 10 against women for procuring (*Source:* Home Office).

Abduction

Another legal route for pursuing men controlling children by acting as their pimps or 'boyfriend' would be to employ the Child Abduction Act 1984. Under Section 2 of the Act, it is an offence for a person to take or keep a child under the age of 16 from the person who is her/his legal guardian. In the case of children in residential or foster care where a care order is in place, the legal guardian would be the local authority. The only defence here is that the man believes he is the child's father or that he believes the child is over 16.

The prosecution would need to prove that a child has been induced to accompany the man or any other person or that the man detained or induced the child to remain with him.

The way forward

Existing legislation needs to be used against offenders which is based on the recognition that the adults who buy sex from children or profit in any way from that exchange are committing serious offences against children. Much of that legislation is in place but requires a difficult task for the police and other agencies assisting in investigation. There is a need to gather sufficient evidence to persuade the CPS that a conviction is possible and that the public interest test is served, given the effects of the crimes on the child victims.

The collation of evidence about pimps controlling children and young people needs to be given much greater emphasis and to be more creative. This is beginning to happen in some police authorities, for example, London's Charing Cross Clubs and Vice Unit which has succeeded in securing convictions against pimps by working with children and young people and by placing more emphasis on proactive investigation of offenders. Many pimps are extremely violent towards the children and young people they control and efforts have been made to support child victims of violence in taking legal action. Again, the fear felt by the child and the control exercised by a pimp means securing conviction can be difficult. Children have the right under Section 43 of the Children Act to refuse physical examination. This could mean that important corroborating evidence is not available. The co-operation of a child will be dependent on many factors, including adequate witness protection arrangements and how the child perceives her/his contact with agencies including police and social services.

With a change in emphasis, it should be possible to pursue pimps for incitement to gross indecency under the Indecency with Children Act 1960 or bring charges under the Sexual Offences Act 1956 relating to sex with children under the legal age of consent. This would have implications for others involved in the abuse of children in this way, for example, landlords and club owners. Under Section 25 of the Sexual Offences Act 1956, it is an offence for an owner, occupier or manager of a premises to knowingly permit girls under 13 to have unlawful sexual intercourse. The maximum penalty is life imprisonment. Section 26 provides for a similar offence for girls under 16 with a maximum penalty of two years.

Legislation relating to pimping, kerb crawling and soliciting needs to be amended so that it is consistent with the Children Act and other legislation aimed at protecting children. The police role is to carry out investigations into alleged or suspected offences but officers can, under

Section 47 of the Children Act, call upon other agencies such as the NSPCC for help in order to carry out investigations. Those agencies are obliged to assist unless it would be unreasonable in the circumstances.

Much of the legislation relating to adults soliciting sex or pimping makes no distinction between whether a child or an adult is involved. This coupled with the lack of investigations into the activities of adult perpetrators leaves children vulnerable to violence and control while child prostitution remains a relatively 'safe option' for male abusers.

THE CHILDREN ACT 1989

The Children Act 1989 ('the Act') provided a new framework for the care and protection of children and established new criteria in relation to child protection. The Act established a legal framework for the protection of children both outside court proceedings and in the context of court proceedings. These areas overlap to some extent but are dealt with under separate headings below.

Outside court proceedings

The provisions contained in Part III of the Act (the title of which is 'Local Authority Support for Children and Families') place a general duty on local authorities to safeguard and promote the welfare of children within their area who are in need; and, so far as is consistent with that duty, to promote the upbringing of such children by their families. Sections 17 to 30 of the Act define the duties of local authorities to safeguard and promote the welfare of children within their area who are in need and Part I of Schedule 2 of the Act provides further amplification and clarification of those duties.

Under Paragraph 4 of Schedule 2, every local authority has a duty to take reasonable steps, through the provision of services under Parts II and III of the Act, to prevent children within its area suffering ill-treatment or neglect.

Paragraph 7 of Schedule 2 states that every local authority shall take reasonable steps to reduce the need to bring proceedings for care or supervision orders with respect to a child within its area and to reduce the need to bring criminal proceedings against children. The same paragraph imposes a duty on local authorities to take reasonable steps to encourage children within their area not to commit criminal offences and to avoid the need for children within their area to be placed in secure accommodation.

The Act provides a local authority with general powers and duties which could ensure that children do not suffer by becoming involved in prostitution. Prostitution is a means of survival for some children who are not protected and supported by their families. The services and support which should be available from local authorities as a result of the Act could and should be used to ensure that children do not become trapped in a life dependent upon prostitution.

The important sections of Part III of the Act, with a brief description of the duties contained in those sections, are set out below.

Section 17

This section imposes a general duty on every local authority to safeguard and promote the welfare of children within its area who are in need by providing an appropriate range and level of services. This section also provides that the local authority shall have the specific duties and powers set out in Part I of Schedule 2 (referred to above). Should a child require certain services which the local authority is not able to provide, this section places a duty on the local authority to arrange for such services to be provided by other agencies. The Act clearly envisages that services should be provided to children in need; for example, accommodation, guidance from social workers and counselling from appropriate professionals.

Section 20

This section places a specific duty on local authorities to provide accommodation for any child in need within their area who appears to them to require accommodation as a result of either there being no person who has Parental Responsibility for her/him (the child being lost or abandoned) or where the person who has been caring for her/him has been prevented from providing her/him with suitable accommodation or care. Parental Responsibility is defined in Section 3 of the Act as 'all the rights, duties, powers, responsibilities and authority which by law a parent of a child has in relation to the child and his property'.

A child reliant upon prostitution for a living might well fall within the definition of 'a child in need' and, accordingly, local authorities are under a duty to provide that child with accommodation.

Section 22

This section places a duty on local authorities in relation to children who are looked after by them. The section states that it shall be the duty of the local authority looking after any child to safeguard and promote her/his welfare. Before making any decisions on behalf of a child being looked after by a local authority, that local authority must, so far as is reasonably practicable, ascertain the wishes and feelings of the child.

Safeguarding and promoting a child's welfare could be achieved by a local authority outside the context of legal proceedings, providing that the child and anyone with Parental Responsibility for the child are agreeable to the local authority's plans. If there is no agreement the local authority may consider, as one of the options, applying for a care order in order to promote the child's welfare.

Section 24

This section places a duty on local authorities to provide after care for young persons over 16 who have been looked after by them up to the age of 21. The section specifically provides that where a child is being looked after by a local authority, it shall be the duty of the local authority to advise, assist and befriend with a view to promoting her/his welfare when s/he ceases to be looked after by the authority. This would involve the local authority ensuring that appropriate professionals assist the young person to make plans for her/his future, including accommodation, education and employment. For a child who has been or may become involved in prostitution, this sort of support is essential as a preventative measure.

Section 46

Part V of the Act, entitled 'Protection of Children', is also important in the context of child prostitution. The police are granted emergency powers under Section 46 of the Act to protect a child who would otherwise be likely to suffer significant harm. The powers given to the police are that a constable may remove such a child to suitable accommodation and keep her/him there or take such steps as are reasonable to ensure that the child's removal from any hospital, or other place, in which s/he is then being accommodated is prevented. Police protection of a child cannot last for more than 72 hours.

As soon as is reasonably practical, a constable who has taken a child into police protection must inform the local authority within the area in which the child was found of the steps that have been, and are proposed to be, taken and the reasons for taking them. The police officer must also give details to the authority within the area the child normally lives of the place at which the child is being accommodated and do the following:

- inform the child (if s/he appears capable of understanding) of the steps that have been taken with respect to her/him and the reasons for taking them, and of the further steps that may be taken.

- Take such steps as are reasonably practicable to discover the wishes and feelings of the child.

- Where the child has been taken into police protection by being removed to accommodation which is not provided by or on behalf of the local authority or a refuge for children (Section 51 of the Act), the police officer should ensure that s/he is moved to accommodation of this nature.

- Ensure that the case is enquired into by an officer designated for that specific purpose. The designated officer should thereafter allow certain categories of person to have contact with the child if appropriate. Requirements for allowing appropriate contact pass to the caring authority if the child has been taken into accommodation provided by the authority.

If a police constable discovers that a child is in circumstances which involve her/him in prostitution, it is open to that officer to use Section 46 of the Act to ensure that immediate steps are taken to protect the child from further harm.

Section 47

This section imposes a duty on local authorities where they are informed that a child lives or is found in their area who is the subject of an emergency protection order or is in police protection, or where they have reasonable cause to suspect that a child who lives or is found in their area is suffering or is likely to suffer significant harm. The duty is then *imposed* upon the local authority to investigate the child's circumstances and decide whether or not to take any action to safeguard or promote the child's welfare.

The investigative process should involve collecting information from other key professionals and communicating with other agencies such as the police or the NSPCC. It is up to the local authority to decide what, if any, action is necessary to protect a child, although any action taken should be in collaboration with other agencies involved with the child. This could include social services being called upon to co-operate in investigations into adult offenders and take a proactive role where it is known that children in local authority care are involved in child prostitution. Although the police may wish to ensure that all appropriate measures are taken for the protection of a child, the final responsibility for ensuring that a child is protected falls on the relevant social services department.

Clearly, the Act, and in particular Part III of the Act, places important statutory duties on local authorities to promote the welfare of children in their area. General guidance on the Children Act sets out in more detail how these services should be delivered. The ways in which local authorities should ensure that they discharge their duties to protect children is set out in official guidance entitled *Working Together under the Children Act 1989: A Guide to Arrangements for Inter-agency Co-operation for the Protection of Children from Abuse*. This publication is produced by the Home Office, Department of Health, Department of Education and Science and Welsh Office, 1991.

Should the local authority not be discharging its statutory duties in the manner required by the Act, any lawyer advising or representing a child in need who is entitled to the services and protection specified in the Act should give consideration to mounting a Judicial Review of the local authority's decision not to provide services or protection.

For example, if a child involved in prostitution has been taken into police protection and is subsequently not accommodated by the local authority and provided with the services the local authority is under a duty to provide as a result of Part III and Schedule 2 of the Act, consideration ought to be given as to whether or not the decision of the local authority not to provide those services is unreasonable (*Associated Provisional Picture Houses Limited* v. *Wednesbury Corporation* [1947] 2 All ER 680).

In the context of court proceedings

The Act sets out important principles to be applied by the court in certain court proceedings relating to children. Those principles are set out in Section 1 of the Act, which is entitled 'Welfare of the Child'. The principles can be identified as follows:

- Section 1 (1) – The child's welfare shall be the court's paramount consideration.

- Section 1 (2) – Any delay in the proceedings in which any question with respect to the upbringing of the child arises is likely to prejudice the welfare of the child.

- Section 1 (3) – This section lists a number of factors which should be taken into account by the court when deciding whether or not to make an order under the Act. The list is often referred to as the 'Welfare Checklist' and the factors are as follows:

(a) the ascertainable wishes and feelings of the child concerned (considered in the light of his age and understanding);

(b) his physical, emotional and educational needs;

(c) the likely effect on him of any change in his circumstances;

(d) his age, sex, background and any characteristics of his which the Court considers relevant;

(e) any harm which he has suffered or is at risk of suffering;

(f) how capable each of his parents, and any other person in relation to whom the Court considers the question to be relevant, is of meeting his needs;

(g) the range of powers available to the Court under this Act in the proceedings in question.

- Section 1 (4) – Provides that the Welfare Checklist shall apply where the court is considering making, varying or discharging an order under Part IV.

- Section 1 (5) – Often referred to as the 'no order' principle, this provision was included in the Act to discourage children being removed from inadequate home circumstances when there is no evidence to suggest a care order would improve the child's situation.

The Act grants powers to local authorities and the NSPCC to apply for orders relating to children in public law with a view to protecting them from harm and promoting their welfare. The sections relevant to a child who may be involved in prostitution are set out below.

Section 44

This section entitles any person to apply to the court for an emergency protection order. The court may only make that order if it is satisfied that there is reasonable cause to believe the child is likely to suffer significant harm if s/he is not removed to accommodation provided by or on behalf of the applicant, or if s/he does not remain in the place in which s/he is then being accommodated.

There is no definition as to the meaning of 'significant' in the Act nor is there official guidance and, while there is much case law relating to this area, it remains a very complicated one. The Act does not say either what it means by 'similar child' but in comparing the health and development of one child with that of another those factors that are intrinsic to the child would certainly include sex, age and race.

If an emergency protection order is granted, the applicant acquires Parental Responsibility under the Act for a time-limited period. The immediate effect of an emergency protection order is usually that the child concerned is placed in local authority accommodation and an investigation into the child's circumstances is conducted with a view to assessing whether or not further legal proceedings are required; for example, an application for a care or supervision order.

Section 45

This section provides that emergency protection orders shall have effect for a period not exceeding eight days in the first instance. In the case of a local authority or the NSPCC, an application can be made for an extension of the period of an emergency protection order for a further seven days. The court may only grant such an extension if it has reasonable cause to believe that the child concerned is likely to suffer significant harm if the order is not extended. The child, parents, those with parental responsibility or any one with whom the child was living immediately before the emergency protection order was made can apply for the order to be discharged after 72 hours have elapsed.

Section 31

Part IV of the Act makes provision for the making and administration of care orders. This is important for children who are at risk and cannot be protected in other ways. Section 31 entitles the local authority or the NSPCC to apply to the court for a care or supervision order. The effect of such an application should it be granted is that the child who is the subject of the proceedings is placed in the care of the designated local authority or under the supervision of that local authority. A court can only make a care or supervision order if it is satisfied:

(a) that the child concerned is suffering, or is likely to suffer, significant harm; and

(b) that the harm, or likelihood of harm, is attributable to:

(i) the care given to the child, or likely to be given to him if the order were not made, not being what it would be reasonable to expect a parent to give to him; or

(ii) the child's being beyond parental control.

This test is often referred to as the threshold criteria.

'Harm' is defined as ill-treatment or the impairment of health or development. 'Development' means physical, intellectual, emotional, social or behavioural development. 'Health' is defined as physical or mental health. 'Ill-treatment' includes sexual abuse and forms of ill-treatment that are not physical.

This section also provides that where the question of whether harm suffered by a child is significant, which turns on the child's health or development, then her/his health or development must be compared with that which could reasonably be expected of a similar child.

There is no jurisdiction for the court to make a care order or supervision order with respect to a child who has reached the age of 17 (or 16 in the case of a child who is married).

An application brought by a local authority for a care order in relation to a child involved in prostitution would, in the authors' opinion, be unlikely to be refused as most family courts/child care professionals would conclude that involvement in prostitution would inevitably cause harm to a child.

Section 33

This section sets out the effect of a care order being made in relation to a child. The most important effect is that the local authority acquires Parental Responsibility for the child and can determine the extent to which a parent or guardian of the child may meet her/his Parental Responsibility for the child.

In addition, no person may change a child's surname or remove her/him from the United Kingdom without either the written consent of every person who has Parental Responsibility for the child or the leave of the court where that child is the subject of a care order.

Section 35

This section defines the effect of a supervision order. If a supervision order is made then it is the duty of the supervisor (usually a social worker) to advise, assist and befriend the supervised child, to take such steps as reasonably necessary to give effect to the order and, where the order is not wholly complied with or the supervisor considers that the order may no longer be necessary, to return the matter to court for a variation or discharge.

Section 35 is linked with Parts I and II of Schedule 3. Schedule 3 sets out the powers of the supervisor when giving directions to a supervised child. A supervision order may require the supervised child to submit to a medical/psychiatric examination and the supervisor may require a supervised child to live at a particular place and to present her-/himself to persons at places and on days specified by the supervisor.

Section 38

This section contains provisions for the making of interim care or supervision orders on the same grounds as ordinary care proceedings.

Section 49

This section provides that a person who abducts a child who is the subject of a care or emergency protection order or is in police protection shall be guilty of an offence and liable to summary conviction to imprisonment to a term not exceeding six months or to a fine not exceeding level 5 on the standard scale, or both.

Abduction includes taking the child away from a responsible person, keeping such a child away from a responsible person or inducing, assisting or inciting such a child to run away or stay away from a responsible person. A responsible person is defined as the person who, for the time being, has care of the child by virtue of a care order, emergency protection order or pursuant to Section 46 of the Act.

A pimp who has incited or assisted a child who is the subject of a care order to run away or stay away from the accommodation provided by a local authority could be charged with an offence under these provisions.

Section 50

This section gives the court power to make an order for the recovery of the child who has been abducted whilst the subject of a care order, emergency protection order or whilst under police protection. A person who has Parental Responsibility by virtue of a care or emergency protection order, or the designated officer in the case of a child in police protection, may make the application for a recovery order. The order grants the following powers to the applicant:

- It operates as a direction to any person who is in a position to do so to produce a child on request to any authorised person.

- It authorises the removal of the child by any authorised person.

- It requires any person who has information as to the child's whereabouts to disclose that information, if asked to do so, to a constable or an officer of the court.

- It authorises a constable to enter any premises specified in the order and search for the child using reasonable force if necessary.

Sections 49 and 50 relate to issues of surveillance, detection and apprehension of adult offenders which are discussed in more detail above.

Section 25

This section deals with the provisions for secure accommodation of children. It provides that a local authority may not place a child in secure accommodation unless it appears that s/he has a history of absconding or is likely to abscond from any other description of accommodation and as a result is likely to suffer significant harm; or, alternatively, that if the child is kept in any other description of accommodation, s/he is likely to injure her-/himself or other persons.

Upon the application of a local authority the court may make an order authorising the child to be placed in secure accommodation and it must specify the maximum period for which the child may be so kept. The court may not make a secure accommodation order if a child is not legally represented in court unless s/he has been informed of her/his right to apply for Legal Aid and, having had an opportunity to do so, has refused and failed to apply.

The use of secure accommodation may be appropriate to prevent a child from being at risk of significant harm if, for example, a child repeatedly absconds to return to the control of a pimp and involvement in prostitution. However, the use of secure accommodation can be viewed by young people as a punitive response and, as its use is time limited, is unlikely on its own to reduce the risks faced by a young person on leaving the secure accommodation.

It can be seen from the outline of the Act set out above that much of the legal framework for responding to children and young people involved in prostitution is already in place. In addition, the Act requires the provision of services for children in need.

Children and young people involved in the sex industry and prostitution may have a range of needs not directly related to their activity on the streets (for example, housing and education). Section 27 enables cooperation between, for example, housing, health and education authorities to help a local authority in the exercise of its functions. Often the failure of local authorities to identify these needs and meet them is a factor in a child's involvement in prostitution.

Similarly, research shows that young people from residential care are over represented amongst those living on the streets. Many children 'leave' the care system before they have reached the age of 16 and as a consequence may not have easy access to the after-care support local authorities are under a duty to provide (Stein *et al.*, 1994). In addition, it is not unusual for children and young people leaving the care system after 16 not to be provided with the services to which they are legally entitled.

The powers granted to local authorities and the NSPCC under the Act, and the provision in the Act for inter-agency work in relation to child protection and emergency intervention in relation to the welfare of children, could (and should in the authors' opinion) be used to ensure that the 'welfare' route is taken in relation to children involved in prostitution. Local authorities should provide services geared to enabling young people who are at risk as a result of their prostitution activities to reject that lifestyle.

SOLICITORS AND THE CHILD CLIENT

Advice and representation

If advising and representing a child involved in prostitution who may be involved in court proceedings, a solicitor should, in our view, take up the role of advocate on behalf of her/his child client and do as much as possible to persuade all involved to divert the child into the welfare route rather than punish her/him for the offence. This is subject to the caveat that the child instructs the solicitor in such a way.

Advising or representing a child client presents new challenges to a solicitor and requires particular skills when taking instructions, advising and representing. The Law Society operates a Children Panel whose members have undergone specialist training and have been assessed by the Panel's interviewers prior to being appointed. As a result, solicitors on the Children Panel should be sensitive to the special requirements of children when they seek legal advice and representation. This is not to say that solicitors who are not Panel members may not or should not advise and represent children, but if they choose to do so they should remain sensitive to their child client's needs and circumstances. Barristers, who are called upon to act in more complex child care cases, are guided by similar principles.

If a solicitor without previous experience of advising or representing a child intends to take on instructions from a child but needs immediate guidance in relation to advising and representing a child client, it is advisable for that solicitor to contact a member of the Children Panel to discuss her/his instructions and how to proceed.

The United Nations Convention on the Rights of the Child was adopted in 1989 and ratified by the United Kingdom in 1991. Article 12 of the Convention states as follows:

1. States Parties shall assure to the child who is capable of forming his or her own views the right to express those views freely in all matters affecting the child, the views of the child being given due weight in accordance with the age and maturity of the child.

2. For this purpose, the child shall in particular be provided the opportunity to be heard in any judicial and administrative proceedings affecting the child, either directly or through a representative or an appropriate body, in a manner consistent with the procedural rules of National Law.

These principles are very much reflected in the Children Act 1989. In addition, the findings of the Report of the Inquiry into Child Abuse in Cleveland (HMSO, 1987) and the decision in the case of *Gillick* v. *West Norfolk and Wisbech Area Health Authority and the Department of Health and Social Security* [1985] FLR 736, very much affected the formulation of the Children Act 1989.

In the Gillick case, the House of Lords decided that the duration of parental rights could not be linked to a child reaching a particular age, but that it was necessary to judge what was best for the welfare of any particular child in particular circumstances on an individual basis.

The Cleveland Report referred to above contains further guidance for those involved in assessing the competence of a child, taking instructions from a child or representing a child in legal proceedings. Some of the specific recommendations of the Cleveland Report are as follows:

- There should be recognition by professionals that children are entitled to a proper explanation and to be given some idea of what is going to happen to them. The explanation should be appropriate to their age and understanding.

- Children should always be listened to carefully by professionals and what they say should be taken seriously.

- If involved in legal proceedings, the views and wishes of the child should be considered carefully by professionals, in particular in relation to what should happen to the child.

- The court dealing with the child's case should have the child's views and wishes placed before it.

- A child should always be interviewed in a sensitive environment suited to her/his needs.

It is not appropriate for a solicitor charged with advising and representing a child to do what s/he thinks is in the child's best interests. The solicitor's role is to be the child's advocate, i.e. to ensure that the child's wishes and feelings are clearly conveyed to those involved with the child and proceedings. A solicitor representing a competent child may find her-/himself in an extremely difficult position where her/his own views about what is in the child's best interests conflict with the child's instructions. Should this happen, for example, where a child discloses that s/he is involved in child prostitution and intends to continue that involvement, the solicitor's duty is still to ensure that the child's case is put as clearly as possible.

Solicitors generally have a duty of confidentiality towards their clients. The Standards and Guidance Committee and the Family Law Committee of the Law Society have issued guidelines for solicitors in dealing with confidential information from a child client. If a solicitor has assessed a child as competent, then the child should be represented in accordance with her/his instructions.

In trying to determine whether to retain confidentiality, solicitors will find it useful to refer to the principles of the Gillick case briefly discussed above. It is necessary to make a judgement based on the child's understanding of the case and in some circumstances it may be appropriate to approach a third party such as a health professional with knowledge of the child for assistance. If it is concluded that a child client is not competent, then the solicitor's duty is to act in the child's best interests. This could involve representing the child through her/his guardian *ad litem* in the context of public law proceedings.

If a competent child discloses information s/he wishes to remain confidential, the solicitor must consider whether or not it is possible to divulge that information to third parties. The first consideration must be whether or not the information is in fact confidential. If the client tells a solicitor something prior to the commission of a crime (with the intention of being helped or guided in the commission of the crime) the information need not be seen as confidential. This is the position in common law. The solicitor in these circumstances would be at liberty to pass the information on to a third party. The consideration for the child's solicitor is therefore whether or not the communication made by the child is in order to be assisted or guided in committing an offence.

In addition, the solicitor has a duty to consider the public interest. For example, if a child gives information about other children being at risk from adult abusers, the solicitor must exercise his discretion whether or not to disclose the confidential information against the child's wishes. If the duty to retain confidentiality is outweighed by the public interest point – the protection of other children at risk – then the solicitor should disclose the information. The duty of confidentiality should never be breached unless there is a strong suspicion that abuse has taken place.

Before taking the decision to disclose confidential information against a competent child's wishes, a solicitor should try to persuade the child to disclose the information to her/his guardian *ad litem* or a social worker. The solicitor could also suggest that s/he is instructed by the child to speak to the guardian *ad litem* or social worker on the child's behalf. Where an immature child who is subject to abuse refuses to allow her/his solicitor to reveal that abuse, any disclosure of information should only be made if it is in the public interest *and* there is no other less oppressive method of dealing with the situation such as the guardian *ad litem* disclosing the abuse. When confidentiality is breached, the child should be informed.

Legal Aid

The Legal Aid scheme is available to children for advice and representation. Advice and assistance is available for children under 16 years of age under the Green Form scheme. In certain public law proceedings (care/supervision proceedings, application for emergency protection and child assessment orders, and applications for discharge of emergency protection orders) non-means, non-merits-tested Legal Aid is available to children. A solicitor representing a child in these proceedings can self-certify and submit the application to the Legal Aid Board. Legal Aid will be granted as of right.

Care proceedings under the Children Act 1989

Should the local authority commence care proceedings in respect of a child who is involved in prostitution, the child is automatically a party to those proceedings.

A guardian *ad litem* will be appointed for the child. The guardian *ad litem* has a duty to advise the court what is in the child's best interests from her/his professional point of view and to ensure that the child's wishes and feelings are conveyed to the court. The guardian *ad litem* is responsible for appointing a solicitor to represent the child.

The solicitor takes her/his instructions from the guardian *ad litem* if the child is not competent to instruct the solicitor direct. Equally, if a competent child's instructions do not differ from the instructions given by the guardian *ad litem*, the solicitor will take her/his instructions from the guardian *ad litem*. If, however, a competent child's instructions to the solicitor conflict with the guardian *ad litem*'s instructions, the solicitor is under a duty to act upon the instructions of the child. In these circumstances, the guardian *ad litem* must decide whether s/he needs legal representation. Even if the solicitor views a child's instructions as contrary to the child's interests, the solicitor must follow those instructions as s/he would do with a competent adult client.

It is the solicitor's duty to assess a child's understanding and the duty is a continuing one throughout the progression of the proceedings. It is also the duty of a solicitor to ascertain from a competent child what her/his wishes and feelings are, and, in relation to the final hearing of the local authority's application, the views of the child on whether or not an order should be made.

Where a child client is not to be present in court (and this is the usual situation) it is important that the solicitor commits her-/himself to performing the role of the child's advocate at the hearing. Child clients are often reassured by the fact that their own solicitor, with whom they have spent time and explained their wishes and feelings, will be presenting their case. Needless to say, those children who are or have been involved in prostitution, and as a result are the subject of public law proceedings, require very committed and energetic representation.

CONCLUSION

Children involved in prostitution who subsequently become involved in legal proceedings face a difficult time. Society can choose either to criminalise children exploited in the sex industry or to attempt to support and protect them. Existing legislation could be used, as suggested above, to protect and support children with a view to diverting them from prostitution and the exploitation of adults. Additionally, criminal legislation could be used to focus on the abusers of children in the context of prostitution. In the authors' opinion neither of the above can be achieved without the other.

If, as it seems, criminal legislation is inadequate to deal with the issue of adults exploiting children, both male and female, through prostitution, thought should be given to amending current legislation or to formulating new legislation to target the exploiters of children rather than punishing those who are exploited.

4. Issues for Voluntary Sector Detached Work Agencies

Cath Hayes and Ian Trafford

> By all means let us address the issues of 'prostitution' as moral issues
> but let us try please to address young 'prostitutes' as people with needs.
> And 'needs' which can be met. (McMullen, 1987)

The purpose of this chapter is to explore some of the issues arising out of face-to-face work with young people involved in prostitution in a detached or streetwork context. In doing this, we will be reflecting on the particular experience of the Safe in the City Project in Manchester. We begin with a broad account of the work of the project focusing on the issues of young people on the streets and those involved in prostitution. The aim here is to identify some of the general issues the project has to address arising out of its work with young people. The next section looks at how the work of the project relates to the statutory framework, with particular reference to the factors that inform its policies and practice guidelines. We then explore in more depth the work with young people on the streets and the practice issues this throws up for the project. We look at some of the advantages and limitations of streetwork as a means of establishing contact with, and offering a service to, young people involved in prostitution and highlight some of the issues and dilemmas that may be faced by workers and agencies. We conclude with some comments about the potential role of streetwork in working with this group of young people and how voluntary agencies might relate to and work in partnership with the statutory sector.

Safe in the City — History, Aims and Objectives

The project was set up by The Children's Society in 1990. The aim of Safe in the City's work is to 'uphold and promote young people's rights, to enable young people to have greater control over their own lives.'

At present, the project mainly works with young people under 18 who are detached from appropriate sources of care and support, and who live on, or spend much of their time on, the streets of Manchester city centre where they may be at risk from various forms of exploitation and abuse. Many of the young people in contact with the project have run away from home or local authority care and much of the work is around helping them to resolve the issues that have led them to run away and helping them to re-establish contact with their families or the care system.

SAFE IN THE CITY AND YOUNG PEOPLE ON THE STREETS

In many ways the young people in contact with Safe in the City could be described as 'street children'. There is much debate around the issue of defining 'street children'. Benno Glauser uses 'street children' as a 'generic term used to refer to a group of children with a special relationship to the street' (Ennew, 1994) and this definition seems appropriate given the lifestyles and experience of the young people in contact with the project.

Recent research carried out by Leeds University looked at the experiences of young people missing from home or care who were in touch with The Children's Society's various streetwork projects (including Safe in the City). It identifies a small group of young people who are, in many cases, almost wholly detached from their families or the care system. They reported running away for a variety of reasons: abuse, violence, family break up, bullying, not feeling cared for, not being listened to. These young people spent much of their time effectively living on the streets. Their primary relationships were with other people living on the streets. Their main sources of food were takeaways and soup runs. They obtained money from street-based activities such as working on the fair, begging, prostitution and acquisitive crime. In the absence of other places to stay they slept rough. Many of these young people retained some contact with their families or with the care system, occasionally returning of their own accord or being returned by the police. However, for the most part they lived on the streets, largely detached from traditional sources of adult care and support (Stein *et al.*, 1994).

Many of the young people with whom Safe in the City works fit this profile of street children. Street children highlight many of the tensions that exist between adult perceptions of idealised childhood and the reality of some young people's lives. They have somehow lost their innocence and point to the apparent failure of individual adults, and society as a whole, to protect children. Such children are often seen as, on the one hand, deviant and in need of either pity, guidance, protection and rescuing or, on the other, in need of discipline, correction and punishment (Ennew, 1994). Such attitudes have characterised media portrayals of young people on the streets and particularly those involved in prostitution. In our experience, such attitudes have also played a large part in the response of statutory agencies such as the police and social services to the needs of these young people.

SAFE IN THE CITY AND YOUNG PEOPLE INVOLVED IN PROSTITUTION

Throughout this chapter the term 'young people involved in prostitution' will generally be used as it more accurately describes the lifestyles and experiences of the young people concerned than terms like 'child prostitutes' or 'juvenile prostitutes'. Prostitution is an aspect of the lives of the young people under discussion but this activity does not, and we would argue should not, define them or their lifestyles. A definition of prostitution which refers to engaging in sexual activity in return for money is both too narrow and misleading. In our experience, young people engage in sex with older men not just for money, but for a range of things including a place to stay, drugs, a lift home, companionship etc. Many of these young people would not define what they do as 'prostitution' because of the stigma attached and this can make it difficult for workers to engage with them about the risks involved.

The term 'prostitute' often implies that the person concerned has made an active and voluntary choice to be involved in prostitution. This is rarely the case for young people or indeed many adults involved in prostitution (Shaw *et al.*, 1996). While it is not the purpose of this chapter to explore the complex reasons that lead young people into prostitution, it is worth making some observations.

An understanding of the factors which precipitate young people's involvement in prostitution is vital for workers who are likely to come into contact with young people in this situation. Although there are many factors which may leave some young people vulnerable to involvement in prostitution, prostitution only exists because there is a demand. It is increasingly being recognised that child prostitution only exists because there are men willing to pay to abuse children. Child prostitution is child abuse. A recent United Nations Commission On Human Rights report defined child prostitution as 'the act of engaging or offering the services of a child to perform sexual acts for money or other consideration with that person or any other person'. The report continues, 'Under this definition, child prostitution is not "committed" by the child itself, but by the person "engaging or offering the services of a child" ' (Calcetas-Santos, 1996).

The factors that leave young people vulnerable to involvement in prostitution mirror the factors which lead young people to end up living on the streets. Abuse, poverty, family breakdown, bad experience of the care system, inadequate after-care services and homelessness are all factors which may push some young people onto the streets and into prostitution (Jesson, 1993; Shaw *et al.*, 1996). In our experience, many young people become involved in prostitution as a means of making enough money to survive in the absence of other legitimate sources of income. Green (1992) supports this view. Peer pressure would also appear to be a significant factor. Young people who run away and end up on the streets of Manchester city centre usually meet other young people in the same situation fairly quickly, generally within a few days. It would appear that young people (particularly young women) who start 'hanging around' with other young people who are already involved in prostitution are more likely to end up 'working' themselves. This may be through peer pressure to contribute financially to the group as a whole or sometimes young people are actively involved in 'pimping' other young people. Vulnerable young people are also recruited into prostitution and actively pimped by older men, although this would appear to be less a feature of the Manchester city centre prostitution scene than it is in other areas. A significant proportion of young people involved in prostitution also get heavily involved in drug and alcohol abuse. For some, this becomes a vicious circle in which drug use is necessary to cope with prostitution and prostitution is the only way of getting enough money together to buy the drugs.

The negative push factors identified above may be common to many young people on the streets, but not all young runaways or young homeless end up involved in prostitution. While on the streets young people may face a variety of risks, but in our experience they also identify a number of positive aspects to being on the streets including excitement, freedom, independence, support from others in the same position, being away from the problems at home or in care and access to money. Young people involved in prostitution may, in spite of the risks, identify a range of factors that keep them involved including: the access to money and the subsequent status and options that brings; a sense of belonging to the prostitute community; and the sense of power and control in a sexual encounter with a 'punter' which may differ from previous experiences of abuse (McMullen, 1987). These are the positive pull factors which may lead a young person to remain on the streets and involved in prostitution in the absence of any other apparent options. For many young people, this situation and the risks they face are often exacerbated by low self-esteem and a sense of hopelessness.

Many of these factors are operating in the lives of the young people in contact with the project. Safe in the City is not a specialised agency working solely with young people in prostitution; it works with young people facing a variety of risks and with a variety of needs. We recognise that prostitution is one aspect of the lives of some of the young people the project is in contact with and that this raises particular issues about their safety which require particular responses from workers.

Legal framework

The Children's Society is a voluntary organisation and its work takes place within the context of relevant child care legislation and statutory responsibilities which are not the same as those of the police and social services. This has the advantage of allowing a high degree of flexibility and creativity in the way the project can work with young people and potentially makes the project more accessible to those young people who may feel let down by or suspicious of statutory agencies. The lack of specific duties and responsibilities, however, also means that the project finds itself operating in grey areas of the law which can be stressful and difficult for staff and make it hard to provide a service to young people which is clear and consistent. The development of clear policies and practice guidelines covering all aspects of the project's work (for example, confidentiality, child protection, streetwork practice, provision of condoms) has been an essential part of the setting up and evolution of Safe in the City. Project policy and practice have been, and continue to be, informed by a variety of factors including:

- the needs of young people in the project's target group;

- safety issues for young people and staff;

- legal duties, responsibilities and liabilities;

- • examples of 'good practice' from other agencies;

- • The Children's Society's values, and its social work policies and procedures;

- • local factors (for example, the need to work in a way which is credible to, and allows for joint working with, other local agencies such as social services).

It is clear that policy and practice guidelines may need to be amended as the above factors change but they will always be within certain parameters such as statutes, official guidance and overall agreed policy. Regular evaluation, consultation with other agencies and, most importantly, feedback from young people are essential in ensuring that this process happens.

A range of legislative factors affects the lives of those young people who are in touch with the project. The Children Act 1989 is perhaps the most significant. In setting out a local authority's duties and responsibilities to young people in its area, including those in need, those at risk and young people in care, the Act has a bearing on the lives of most of the young people in contact with Safe in the City. The majority of the young people are or have, at some point in their lives, been looked after by the local authority. In working with and advocating on their behalf, staff need to be aware not only of the relevant legislation, but also how it is interpreted and implemented at a local level.

The work that The Children's Society does with young people is extremely diverse, however the issues of child abuse and child protection are an ever-present concern. Under Section 47 of the Children Act 1989 social services have a duty to investigate where a child is suffering, or is thought to be at risk of suffering, significant harm. There is an expectation informed by Area Child Protection Procedures that other local authority workers, including teachers and youth workers, will disclose information to social services and co-operate in child protection investigations where they believe a child to be at risk of significant harm. As a voluntary organisation, The Children's Society and its projects do not share the same statutory duties with regard to child protection. The Society does operate confidentiality and child protection policies covering the work of its projects in the various different contexts in which they work. However, in general, non-statutory agencies are under no statutory duty to disclose confidential information (Children's Legal Centre, 1992).

PRACTICAL RESPONSE AND PRACTICE ISSUES

Streetwork

There are many parallels between 'streetwork' and 'detached work' and these methods of working have become increasingly significant within youth work. Central to both is the idea of establishing contact with and working with young people on their own territory and on their terms. Detached work, in a broader context, has increasingly been used as a means of establishing contact with people who are not in contact with mainstream centre-based services and who are, perhaps for a variety of reasons, unlikely to use those services. This has particularly been a feature of projects working with people involved in prostitution. Much HIV prevention work with the prostitute community is carried out by means of detached (or outreach) work, with projects providing advice and information, condoms, clean injecting equipment and even medical services to people in the areas in which they are working (Casey *et al.*, 1995).

Safe in the City describes its model of practice as 'streetwork' rather than 'detached'. The project has an office base but most of the direct work with young people takes place on the streets. The term 'streetwork' arises both out of the methodology and the fact that most of the young people in contact with the project are either living on the streets or spend most of their time on the streets of central Manchester. There are many practice issues arising out of the project's work with young people on the streets and some of these have been touched upon above. In the forthcoming sections, we will give an overview of the project's practice while focusing particularly on issues to do with harm reduction, confidentiality and child protection.

Location

The project's streetwork occurs mainly in Manchester city centre, and particularly the areas where young people congregate, including the rail and bus stations, the amusement arcades, the park and the red-light area. Manchester city centre has a well-established and highly visible red-light area, with both men and women working in street prostitution in the same location.

Streetwork practice

Safe in the City has a streetwork team of five. Project workers go out in pairs, usually on a three-hour streetwork session. The project operates 'core times' which are fixed times (half an hour) when project workers will be in particular locations in the city centre, so that young people can turn up and know that they will be able to talk to a worker. The core times are advertised on contact cards which give general information about the project and are given out to young people by workers. These cards are also available in other agencies used by young people, such as the network of day centres in the city centre. Young people can also contact the project by telephone during office hours. Streetwork takes place both during the day and late into the evening.

Equal opportunities

The project has contact with a diverse group of young people, many of whom have particular support needs arising out of their life experience, race, gender, sexuality, ability, etc. The project aims to be as accessible as possible to all the young people in its target group and respond appropriately to their needs. However, this is not always possible and staff will often signpost young people to other appropriate agencies for additional specialist support. Practice issues relating to sexuality and gender, in relation to work with young people involved in prostitution, will now be briefly examined.

Wherever possible, the streetwork pair will be either mixed gender or two women in order to ensure that young women have the option of being able to discuss issues with a female worker. This is particularly important in the red-light area, where a young woman who is working might feel quite intimidated if approached by two men. If two male workers are doing streetwork and establish contact with a new young woman who is working, they may engage very briefly and let her know that a female worker will be out the following day. There are also issues around the assumptions a young man who is working will make if approached by two male workers.

The red-light area is in the same location as Manchester's 'Gay Village', where most of the gay pubs and clubs are located. The project works with young lesbian, gay and bisexual people on the streets who may have been forced to leave home because of their sexuality. It is important that staff have a clear awareness and understanding of issues related to sexuality. These young people often feel more at ease talking issues through with a lesbian or gay worker. The male prostitution ('rent') scene also has its own culture and it is important for workers not to make assumptions about the sexuality or life experience of young men who are working. In our experience, some of the young men are upfront and positive about their gay sexuality and about the fact that they are working the beat. As a consequence, it can be relatively easy to engage with them on issues of safety and sexual health. Other young men who are working and are not 'out' are more difficult to work with. These young men are potentially more at risk, and it is much harder for workers to gain enough trust to engage with them and discuss issues around safety, safer sex and sexual health. One way of doing this can be to offer condoms and talk about sexual health in a way which doesn't make assumptions about the gender of the person they are having sex with.

The police

The work of the project is known to the police. There are regular liaison meetings with senior police officers and senior managers from Manchester Social Services. The purpose of liaison meetings is to explore broad policy issues and not to discuss issues relating to individual young people. During streetwork sessions, project workers will try to keep contact with the police to a minimum in order not to arouse mistrust among the young people.

The red-light area tends to be heavily policed with regular 'purges' (operations to clamp down on the level of prostitution) and this has a number of implications for young people, as it has for older sex workers. Apart from their fears about being arrested for prostitution, some of the young people may be reported missing to the police, may have a warrant outstanding for their arrest, or may be on bail conditions, which exclude them from the city centre. A heavy police presence may force them to work on the fringes of the beat, where they are more isolated and therefore more at risk. They may even move out of town altogether and work in the other red-light areas in Manchester where they don't have the same access to services such as Safe in the City, the day centres and Manchester Action on Street Health (MASH, a specialist service for sex workers).

The police do caution and arrest young people under the age of 18 for soliciting. Streetwork staff could intervene when a young person has been stopped by the police for soliciting and attempt to dissuade the police from arresting or cautioning, reminding the police of the age of the young person and hence their primary duty to protect that young person from harm (Lee and O'Brien, 1995). However, project workers at Safe in the City have rarely had the opportunity to intervene in this way as this requires workers to be on the scene at the precise moment of arrest.

Staff safety

In a detached or streetwork setting, staff are isolated and potentially vulnerable. However, the quality of the relationship built with young people and adults on the street is a significant factor here and this can ensure that workers are trusted and thus reduce the level of risk. It is impossible to eliminate all potential risks and there have been occasions where staff have been threatened. Project staff always work in pairs during streetwork or when going to meet a young person on the streets. This is both for the protection of young people and staff. Each streetwork pair carries a mobile phone and has the option of being able to talk a situation through with the 'on call' line manager.

Threatening situations are relatively rare but the work remains demanding and stressful. The establishment of clear policies and practice guidelines which provide staff with a clear framework within which to operate are vital in minimising the level of stress which staff face. Team meetings, peer support, regular supervision and the option of external counselling are all important mechanisms used in Safe in the City for supporting staff.

BASIC PRINCIPLES

- HOLISTIC

- YOUNG PERSON CENTRED

- EMPOWERING

THE PROCESS

ESTABLISHING CONTACT
↓
BUILDING A RELATIONSHIP
↓
ADVICE, INFORMATION, SUPPORT
↓
HARM REDUCTION
↓
LISTENING AND EXPLORING STRATEGIES
↓
SUPPORTING YOUNG PERSON MOVING OUT OF PROSTITUTION

Figure 1: Safe in the City's streetwork model

Any work with young people on the streets is a process and the model above, Figure 1, represents this. The nature of the process and its duration will be different for each young person. Young people involved in prostitution will often experience all the 'negative pushes', 'positive pulls' and blocks to moving off the streets outlined above. They are likely to be cautious about involvement with any agency. The fact that voluntary sector detached workers can operate with a high degree of flexibility and work in the young people's own territory enhances the potential for developing positive relationships. Building a good relationship is the foundation for any work with a young person. Part of that foundation is gaining the young person's trust by listening to them, respecting them, responding to their needs, and being clear about what they can expect from the agency. A high level of confidentiality is also vital in developing a trusting relationship.

Project workers at Safe in the City will offer advice and information to young people around a variety of issues including their rights in care, housing options, benefits, sexual health, etc. The principle here is to give young people the means to make informed choices. Workers will often be involved in advocating with and on behalf of a young person with their family, carers, social worker, accommodation provider or other agencies. The aim of this advocacy may be to help a young person resolve the issues that have led them onto the streets and into prostitution or to open up opportunities for moving off the streets and gaining access to appropriate accommodation, support and other services.

Harm reduction

Workers at Safe in the City are often faced with the scenario where a young person remains involved in prostitution and is unwilling, or feels unable, to engage with any of the exit strategies that might be available. This presents a dilemma for workers, not least because of the level of risk a young person faces. Living with the fact that a young person may choose (albeit within an apparently limited range of options) to remain involved in prostitution is an uncomfortable position for the project and its staff to be in. Accepting this reality, a 'harm reduction' approach informs much of the work with young people.

Sometimes harm reduction work is quite narrowly focussed. For example, harm reduction work with prostitute women is often about infection control, specifically controlling the spread of HIV. At its best, harm reduction has a more holistic focus and this is the approach that Safe in the City tries to follow in its work with young people on the streets. This means, in terms of sexual health, that harm reduction is not just about giving a young person the resources to practise safer sex (for example, condoms); it also involves working with young people on issues like building self-esteem and confidence so that they may feel more able to negotiate safer sex with a 'punter' or their partner. Harm reduction might be about getting the young person to consider the type of sex they are prepared to engage in, where their engagement with a 'punter' happens and the importance of negotiating these things before getting into a car. It may involve encouraging the young person to get a friend to take down the registration numbers of the cars they get into and inform the 'punter' that this is happening.

Project workers will give condoms and advice about sexual health to young people, in line with the spirit of the Gillick judgement regarding competency, on the basis that they may engage in unsafe sex and that, as a consequence, the young person's health and welfare may be at risk. Project workers would try to avoid supplying condoms on a regular basis and would always encourage a young person to seek advice and contraception from a doctor, a family planning clinic or a young persons' clinic.

The welfare of the young person is paramount within any harm reduction strategy. Harm reduction is an important element of the work given the risks that the young people face, but it is not the end in itself.

Confidentiality and child protection

Confidentiality is vital to the process of developing a relationship with a young person and the fact that they can talk to workers in confidence is highly valued by the young people. In the absence of being able to provide a confidential service, it is unlikely that young people would engage with workers to the extent that they do. Very often the first thing that a young person will ask when they meet workers is, 'you're not going to tell anyone where I am are you?'. Key principles behind Safe in the City's confidentiality policy are that:

- the child/young person is a person in their own right and not an object of concern;

- we must listen carefully to what a young person has to say and take it seriously.

The project is not protective or secretive about its work with young people. Workers will always encourage young people to use the range of agencies that are available to them. If a young person is on the run from home or care, workers will encourage them to at least contact their family or social worker to let them know that they are OK, or allow the worker to do it on their behalf. Workers are acutely aware of the risks young people face on the streets and would offer support in helping a young person resolve the issues that have led them to run away so that they could return to a place of safety. However, this is not always possible. Young people don't run away without a reason. Some are at risk in the places they have left, others feel unhappy and uncared for and see little to be gained by returning. Young people involved in prostitution tend to be very detached and Safe in the City is sometimes the only agency they have any regular contact with.

However, the project does not offer complete confidentiality, in part because this would limit the potential responses of the agency in working with young people at risk. There are exceptional circumstances in which the project would consider breaching confidentiality. These are:

- when a young person is clearly not in control of their own safety, for example, involved in an accident, suffering from a drug overdose, being held against their will, etc;

- when the emotional or mental state of the young person is such that it puts their own, or third parties', lives or safety at risk;

- when a third party is at risk of abuse, for example, a sibling left within a family and being abused;

- when an allegation of misconduct is made against a member of project staff – this would be reported to a senior manager in The Children's Society for it to be properly investigated.

It is important for workers to be clear with a young person at the initial point of contact about the confidentiality policy and the exceptional circumstances, so they have a choice about the amount of personal information they give. If workers feel that the level of risk a young person faces is such that exceptional circumstances prevail, they will always consult with a senior manager before any action is taken. Usually, the whole team will meet to share information and decide on the most appropriate response. If possible, workers will contact the young person in question, inform them of the level of concern for their safety and give them the opportunity to engage with workers in order to move out of the situation they are in. This may not always be possible, for example, if the young person has overdosed or the project becomes aware that a young person is being held against their will. If the project decides to make a child protection referral or raise concerns about a young person's safety with social services, project workers will offer ongoing support and advocacy to the young person if they want it. Often, raising concerns with social services will not result in an immediate change in the young person's situation and workers will endeavour to continue to engage with them. This is likely to be difficult as they may no longer trust the project staff.

Most young people living on the streets face significant risks. Young people involved in prostitution are by definition being abused and are therefore suffering significant harm under the terms of the Children Act, although few local Area Child Protection Procedures specifically include child prostitution as part of their remit (Lee and O'Brien, 1995). If the project were to disclose information based on this threshold, it would in effect be unable to offer a confidential service as most of the young people in contact with the project are at risk of significant harm. In making a decision about whether a young person's situation brings them into the exceptional circumstances with regard to confidentiality, an assessment is made not just about the level of risk, but also the young person's competence, understanding and ability to make changes in the situation they are in. There are parallels here with the Gillick principle, in which the young person's understanding and competence are the tests for workers in being able to offer a confidential service.

It is important to stress that the project is not passive or *laissez faire* in its response to young people at risk. Workers seek to engage with young people about the risks they face with the aim of helping them to reflect on the situation they are in and minimise the risks. Hopefully, a young person will choose to move out of prostitution but this might be a long process. The experience of Safe in the City is that a child or young person centred approach is the most effective. An intervention which is designed to protect a young person but which does not respect their views and wishes is likely to be seen by them as punitive. This is particularly significant in relation to child prostitution where the use of criminal proceedings against under 18s is often defended on the basis that it can provide a route into the child protection process. In our experience, if a young person feels listened to, respected and in control they are more likely to engage with workers and engage with a process of moving on.

Breaching confidentiality (for example, by getting the police to pick a young person up) is rarely going to effect positive changes in that person's situation and is likely to damage the relationship workers have with them and leave the young person further isolated. In our experience, the police regularly pick young people up and return them home or to care, but more often than not, they run away again the following day. Returning a young person without addressing the issues that are leading them to run away is of little value.

MULTI-AGENCY RESPONSE

The young people under discussion here are a diverse group in terms of the factors that have led them into prostitution, their experience of prostitution and the needs they have. As with other young people on the streets, they will often have a variety of needs which might include safe accommodation, a regular income, access to health services and counselling, drugs services, independent advocacy, etc. It is clear that a number of agencies may need to be involved in meeting the needs of a young person involved in prostitution. The role of voluntary sector street-based agencies is significant here. Projects such as Safe in the City are ideally placed to establish initial contact with and build trusting relationships with young people at risk on the streets. From this starting point, such projects can work with a young person in identifying the needs that they have and help them access the appropriate services to meet those needs which the street-based agency is not in a position to address. Safe in the City has developed good networks with a number of other agencies providing services to young people in Manchester so that young people in contact with the project can be referred to the appropriate agency for any specialist help they may need.

A variety of agencies may come into contact with young people involved in prostitution, including the police, the courts, social services, health services, the youth service, voluntary sector projects, etc. These agencies often have quite distinct roles and responsibilities in their contact with young people. It is increasingly being recognised that there needs to be a more co-ordinated response to both the prevention of young people's involvement in prostitution and in making effective interventions with young people already involved (Lee and O'Brien, 1995; Shaw *et al.*, 1996).

A move towards this response has begun in Manchester with a series of multi-agency meetings co-ordinated by the Law Society. The agencies involved include Greater Manchester Police, Social Services, Safe in the City, Manchester Action on Street Health (MASH), Healthy Gay Manchester (a sexual health service for gay men), the City Centre Project (which provides a range of advice, information and support services for young people in the city centre) and other voluntary projects which have contact with young people involved in prostitution in the city. A report has recently been produced for this forum which analyses the current responses being made and makes recommendations for the way forward in terms of intervention strategies and effective inter-agency working. The report is currently under discussion by the agencies concerned and by the Area Child Protection Committee. It remains to be seen what the outcomes of these discussions will be, but there is a clear commitment on the part of all the agencies involved to move towards a better response to young people involved in prostitution and those at risk of becoming involved.

SUMMARY AND CONCLUSION

Young people involved in prostitution are in many ways no different from other young people and share the same need for love, care, respect and support. They share much in common with other young people living on the streets in terms of the factors that have led them to their current position, the risks they face, the needs they have and the blocks they face to moving on. However, young people involved in prostitution do face particular risks and are often especially isolated from potential sources of help and support. Safe in the City attempts to respond to this complex picture by working with young people in a way which seeks to be holistic and young person centred. The starting point is to work with the issues that the young people themselves identify and to move at their pace.

Young people involved in prostitution are a stigmatised, marginalised and criminalised group and are likely to be mistrustful of any intervention, particularly if it is perceived as moralising or coercive. It may take some time to develop a positive and productive relationship with a young person, and the process of working with them until they feel able to move out of prostitution may be a long one. A high degree of confidentiality is vital if young people are going to trust workers enough to engage in that process.

A range of responses is required to prevent young people ending up on the streets and involved in prostitution. This will require some fundamental changes in the systems and structures that affect young people.

It will also require agencies, both statutory and non-statutory, to work together to prevent young people becoming vulnerable to involvement in prostitution.

Similarly, a range of responses is required to meet the needs of young people already involved in prostitution (Shaw *et al.*, 1996). The particular needs of a young person will vary depending on the factors that led them into prostitution and on their background, gender, race, sexuality, motivation, and experience of prostitution. It is clear that no single agency has the power, resources or ability to respond effectively to the diverse experience and needs of these young people. Voluntary sector detached and/or streetwork agencies have a key role to play. They are able to establish contact and work with marginalised young people on the streets who may be detached from all other sources of care and support. The freedom from statutory duties and responsibilities enables such agencies to develop effective relationships with vulnerable young people and work with them in a way which is flexible and responsive. It is vital, however, that this is within an agreed framework of clear policies and procedures. This model of working is not without its frustrations and dilemmas and it can bring streetwork projects into conflict with statutory agencies such as the police and social services. No agency can operate in a vacuum. There is a need for agencies to work together in responding effectively to young people's involvement in prostitution. This means that voluntary sector projects have to develop policies and practice that are clear and credible. It also means that the statutory agencies such as social services need to acknowledge and respect the role that the voluntary sector projects can play in responding to the needs of young people at risk.

All the agencies involved need to have as their starting point an approach which respects and upholds young people's rights. Often young people end up involved in prostitution in the context of a life experience in which they have not been cared for, listened to or respected. Any response which does not empower young people by listening to, respecting and responding to their views and wishes is likely to prove ineffective.

5. Child Prostitution: An Educational Perspective

David Bowen

The role in child prostitution for those engaged in the education of children impinges at all stages: prevention, management and restoration. That, of course, is only in professional terms. There are personal issues involved as well for it should not be forgotten that for the majority who take up teaching or work elsewhere in the education service, the prime motive is to make the lives of children better and more fulfilled. There may be strong feelings evoked by the very notion that children and young people can find themselves compelled or drawn into prostitution, which is, after all, a form of sexual abuse. Indeed, there may even be an unwillingness to acknowledge that such things happen. Yet, as has been seen clearly from the statistical evidence, they do (Lee and O'Brien, 1995).

Many teachers will have direct experience of working with pupils who have suffered such abuse. However, for the majority, while there may be a theoretical understanding, the reality, when it is faced, will be new. The response of teachers to this reality, as it affects individual pupils, is crucial to the future help which the pupil may get and so clearly needs.

There was a similar reaction in the early 1980s when the extent of child sexual abuse first came to attention. Teachers were unwilling to hear what their pupils were saying. The behaviour was outside the school and outside the experience of most who worked with children. If it happened at all, it was rare. It was a matter involving strangers. No mother would tolerate such interference within the family. No respectable father figure would seek to misuse his position. The girl (almost always it was seen as a girl's problem) must accept some of the responsibility, if not the blame. It was certainly not the sort of thing that went on within 'our' families. It is clear, however, that all these assumptions were wrong.

Child sexual abuse is common; generally takes place within the family; may be causing unimaginable emotional strain on the mother; can be found in the most 'respectable' of families; and is never, under any circumstances, the fault of the child, be they boy or girl (Finklehor, 1986).

Child prostitution needs to be seen by the teacher, the educational psychologist, the education welfare officer, youth worker or whoever from within the world of education, as another manifestation of child abuse. While we are still very uncertain about the frequency of child prostitution, experience with every other form of child abuse suggests it is more common than we believe. Discussion within educational circles, such as may be prompted by this book, will help reveal the true size of the problem. While we, perhaps, understand that child prostitution takes place with runaways and drug abusers, it may be less acceptable that parents and carers may prostitute their children, of either sex, for money and their vicarious pleasure. To hear that the girl who vanished from home and school last term has been found working as a prostitute in a nearby city may not surprise the experienced teacher. It may be harder to understand the circumstances which have placed a current pupil in similar behaviour. However, only through understanding the causes can help begin to be provided.

Two regular members of an inner-city youth club, boys of 14, regularly earned considerable sums of money as rent boys. They were not gay. Their sole object was cash. To the boys concerned, what they were doing was no more than an alternative to theft. They knew, but chose to ignore, the risks to their health and safety. There were, inevitably, effects on their education. These two boys were more 'streetwise' than their peers. They showed less interest in their education; their minds were elsewhere, earning or spending. They were unconcerned about their own futures because the present was exciting, rewarding and their own. Apparently mature, they were learning to use other people and not to work with them. Their power over adults was significant and certainly different. They did not fit in with society's expectation of young people of that age and, consequently, its educational regime did not fit comfortably with them either.

A moralistic approach from the school would have offered nothing to these boys. Their family background, in which people were valued for what they owned rather than for what they were, created a climate in which they had no respect for either themselves or others. Success was equated solely with ownership. As children, they were owned by their parents. The family role models were people who were perceived to have money and power within the community. Without these attributes people, especially men, were seen as failures.

No education can take place without being placed in the context of the life of the student or pupil. Education, like social work, starts from where the child is. Unless educators know that genesis, they cannot approach their task with confidence. Of course, in a state-provided system of mass education, it is not possible that provision will make a perfect fit with every pupil. Assumptions have to be made, based on the most common circumstances. There is some scope for adjustment for the individual but only within defined limits. Thus, certain behaviour in school is acceptable and presented by the majority of pupils. Outside that normalcy, for some pupils, according to their needs and abilities, there is a leeway. Beyond that, the school is not expected to make provision and alternative arrangements are, at least in theory, made available. There is a variation from school to school but there is a basic expectation of what is acceptable. When a child veers too far away from that expectation, for whatever reason, something different needs to happen.

There are certain assumptions made about pupils' knowledge of relationships, sexual behaviour and worldliness. Those assumptions are reflected in the curriculum, in the organisation of the school and in the allocation of responsibilities within it. None of those assumptions take child prostitution into account. Nor should they, in general, because to do so would accept that it is a normal part of our society. However, unless educators are prepared to acknowledge that activities which go so clearly against the norms of society do exist and that they involve the children being taught in our schools, they will not be able to tailor the education on offer to those children, comparatively few though they may be, who are involved in the sale of sex.

The Education Acts, the legal framework under which education is provided by the community for children and made compulsory to underline its importance, are all written in the singular. They refer to children as individuals: 'the child' rather than 'children'. It is therefore incumbent on educators of all sorts to try as far as possible to accommodate the needs of each child as a separate being. There is an expectation, supported by law, that teachers undertake a quasi-parental role towards their pupils while they are in their charge. This is most often referred to in the context of disciplinary action. However, it is much wider than this negative approach. Teachers have a duty of care towards their pupils. This was strengthened by the Children Act 1989. It cannot, therefore, be ignored by an educator if it is known or believed that a pupil is engaged in child prostitution. To do so would be a dereliction of duty by a parent and consequently by any other adult with responsibility for the child. It would also be a breach of the UN Convention, Article 34, which states:

> States Parties undertake to protect the child from all forms of sexual exploitation and sexual abuse. For these purposes States Parties shall in particular take all appropriate national, bilateral and multilateral measures to prevent:
>
> (a) the inducement or coercion of a child to engage in any unlawful sexual activity;
>
> (b) the exploitative use of children in prostitution or other unlawful sexual practices;
>
> (c) the exploitative use of children in pornographic performances and materials.

Teachers and others involved in education have, however, two possible responses. Either they can apportion blame and look to the criminal justice system to deal with the problem or they can invoke the protective and rehabilitative processes of the Children Act. A government circular (Department for Education and Employment, Circular 10/95) outlines its expectations of schools and local education authorities in child protection matters. There is to be an acceptance of what children say, an awareness of the problem, training in recognition and procedures for referral to specialist help. The curriculum is to be considered as a preventative tool, reducing secrecy and promoting good relationships. Yet child prostitution remains on the fringe of the child protection process. It is mentioned in passing, usually as a consequence of sexual abuse, in the texts aimed at teachers (for example, Maher, 1987).

Education is not alone in that attitude. There is very little written about the issue and consequently it has a very low profile (if any at all) among those who work with children (Jesson, 1993). Instead, as *The Game's Up* (Lee and O'Brien, 1995) showed, the criminal justice route, based on judgemental attitudes long abandoned in other forms of child sexual abuse, is often used. The consequence for education is that children who have been drawn along that legalistic path are bracketed, like some other criminals, as unwanted in our society. They are likely to be denied the help and support they need from a variety of sources, including education. Schools have become major players in the protection of children from other forms of sexual abuse and can be a realistic force for improvement in the specialised field of child prostitution.

Because children spend so much of their time in school, with responsible and caring teachers, they are learning that schools can be helpful in protecting them from continuing abuse outside school. Schools need to extend the principles and practices that they adopt in that context to child prostitution. First, it is important to accept that a problem exists and that its size is still unknown. It is important to hear what the child says without judgement and in a way that encourages confidence. Referral processes to the social services department need to be in place in such a way that teachers and social workers know and trust each other.

Every local education authority is part of the Area Child Protection Committee (ACPC). This is the body established to co-ordinate action to protect children from all sorts of abuse. Many ACPCs also have teachers as members, recognising the important relationship between pupils and teachers. Teacher members do not come to the ACPC as delegates but as typical of their profession. The ACPC will produce guidelines for handling concerns about child protection issues. Those guidelines should be supplemented by guidance to schools from the local education authority, and by the school's own procedures. All three sets of guidance must work in unison if children are to be afforded the maximum protection. They must contain clear procedures for obtaining help for pupils about whom there is concern. However, procedures will work only as well as those people required to implement them.

It is important that teachers work with their colleagues in the social services department who have prime responsibility in law for child protection. That close working relationship will only come through regular, personal contact. As well as a formal referral procedure, which should involve as short a chain as possible and take as little time as is consistent with proper information being exchanged, there needs to be a willingness to speak informally to each other. Joint training helps with this. The Department for Education and Employment (DfEE) requires training for a designated teacher in each school. In primary schools this is often the head. However, it is the class teacher who has the daily and regular contact with pupils. It is the class teacher who notices changes, who knows the pupil best and, most importantly, is known best by the pupil. Where it has been possible to dedicate some of the school's time for in-service training to child protection issues, involving local colleagues from the social services department, relationships have been seen to be better between the two professions. Attendance at reviews, where time is spent making plans for a particular child, can also help break down the barriers that still exist in some places. When schools wait for a crisis before talking to social workers, relationships are often strained through a lack of trust and mutual ignorance of procedures, responsibilities and capabilities.

Attitudes which see child prostitution as a criminal activity on the child's part should be set aside, as they have been with other forms of abuse, for it is an abuse of adult power, no matter how that power be expressed, which allows a child to sell sexual favours. In particular, schools need to recognise that when a child has been involved in the dehumanising relationships which child prostitution creates, it is through the normalising influence of education that the child victims can both retain and find security and respect.

It is important for teachers to begin by seeing their pupils in their own context. While school is a major influence in a child's life, it is the family in which she or he grows up that sets the foundations of future life. All those who work with children need to be sensitive to the relationships that their charges have at home. Where these are poor, the teacher has an opportunity to offer alternatives. Teachers need to be aware of the outline of their pupils' social lives. If these are mostly focused around older people, especially if there appears to be an unexpected amount of money available, it may be cause for concern, to be shared with colleagues in other agencies. Unexpected knowledge of sexual matters, and an overmature attitude towards them, are also reasons to be concerned. Abuse in early life, because it can so easily damage a child's self-perception, should not be forgotten but should rather be recognised as a long-term problem, even when the child seems to have been rescued from it. (The services for identification and protection are much more advanced than those for treatment and therapy.) Poverty, neglect by those expected to provide care, unrealistic expectations of the child's ability to be self-supporting and acute family breakdown may also tend to drive a child into prostitution (Stein *et al.*, 1994).

Even if the teacher is very sensitive, very aware of the child's problems outside school and anxious to help, it is not always possible to establish the relationship of trust required to gain the pupil's confidence sufficiently to ensure that real help is available. This sort of frustration is experienced by all those who work with children in difficulties. Persistence, and the open and non-judgemental attitudes which all help with the demands of such problems, are the only things available on occasions like these.

Let us look at an example. Mary is 14, lives with her mother and younger brother in a large town in an English shire county and has refused to attend school at all for the past year. She is the subject of an education supervision order and receives tuition for a few hours each week from a home tutor appointed by the education authority. Her education is no more than a matter of form. Her supervisor, an experienced and very caring Education Welfare Officer (EWO), believes that Mary's mother earns her living as a prostitute. She also believes that Mary does the same, but without her mother's knowledge, in order to buy alcohol. It seems clear to the EWO that the local police are aware of the activities of both mother and daughter. Neither they nor the EWO have taken any action to deal with Mary's problem. The EWO does not know what to do. This is not a situation she has recognised before.

Until such time as Mary comes to trust the EWO and is open to change, all that can be done for her is to accept her situation, perhaps trying to minimise risks, adopt a non-judgemental attitude which values Mary but not her behaviour and explore the causes with her. It is likely that she can see no alternative available. She may well have consigned herself to a role in life which, while not her choice, she accepts as her lot. This lack of self-esteem is the first thing that needs to be changed. So long as young women like Mary think little of themselves, they cannot make decisions about taking control of their own lives in a positive way.

Many working in education have seen 'overmature' girls, socially adept, clearly in control of their lives, who have dropped out of school. Some attend sporadically, some do not attend at all. They are often vague about what they do in these absences. They seem to have adult friends. It is very rare that a teacher or an EWO will consider that the girl is engaged in prostitution but it needs to be recognised that there is a real possibility that it is going on. Schools and education authorities must be assiduous in following up absences, not just to collect excuses but to establish genuine causes and, where there are problems, to help find solutions to them.

Absence from school has many causes, perhaps as many as there are absentees. When schools fail to respond to the social as well as the educational needs of their pupils, it is hardly surprising that the pupils elect to be elsewhere as we have seen recently with truancy rates (Brodie and Berridge, 1996). Pupils mature at different rates. Adolescence is a difficult time for everyone involved. The setting of realistic and understandable boundaries provides a framework which all young people need if they are to have any sense of security through these difficult years. However, those boundaries must, if they are to be effective, recognise and respect the individuality of each pupil. Schools can afford a safe place in which to grow up but only if there is someone within them to whom troubled pupils can turn. The pastoral system, however any particular school may decide to organise it, should afford every pupil the opportunity of knowing a responsible adult well, of being known as a person in turn, and offer a non-judgemental and supportive atmosphere in which problems can be shared and help found. The escalation of the school exclusion phenomenon (Brodie and Berridge, 1996) only serves to further marginalise pupils from support systems.

Bullying is regularly identified by pupils as a problem. For some it is a severe problem. For a few it is so severe that drastic action is taken: running away or even suicide. Yet there are approaches which have been tested and shown to help with its solution. A line which offers no blame to either side but emphasises the respect to which every person is entitled, which demonstrates to the bully the pain they are causing, which understands the helpless position of the victim, is more likely to be effective than a punitive and legalistic approach. Bullying is an often quoted reason for running away (Stein *et al.*, 1994). If a pupil takes that route, how will they maintain themselves? There are few legitimate courses of action open. An apparently easy way in which to earn cash is through prostitution. Schools can help protect children from its effects by taking bullying seriously.

To do so, they need to hear what pupils are saying about their social interactions in school. They need to make it safe for pupils to talk. They need to listen and believe what they are told. Exactly the same prerequisites occur when considering child abuse. Because child sexual abuse destroys the self-respect of the victim, it makes it easier to move into prostitution. It is of the utmost importance that, in their responses to the requirements of Circular 10/95 from the DfEE, schools provide training for all staff. That training should always include an emphasis on the need for teachers and others to pick up early signals, to listen carefully to what is being said or not said and to seek advice whenever there is any doubt.

Donovan (1991) records the story of a man of 19. From a family of limited intellectual ability, and having special educational needs himself, he dropped out of school. 'I was forcibly buggered when I was 13 by men who were members of a gang. After that I became a full-time rent boy'. We do not know from Donovan's work if the man concerned had tried to talk to anyone after the initial assault. We do not know what attempts were made to follow up his absence from school. However, it is hard to believe that a school which cares for and knows its pupils well would fail to notice the changes in behaviour and attitude which such a violent assault must have produced. How significant was the low ability of the family and the boy himself? Did it contribute towards a reluctance to 'hear' what was being said?

What is certain is that this young man had contracted Hepatitis B. He also ran other risks. 'Unemployed, homeless, ex-offending young people are at a higher risk of finding themselves involved in HIV risk behaviour' (Pritchard, 1995). The formal curriculum in schools has a genuinely preventative role here. The science curriculum should contain information about HIV; however, that is of little use unless it is put in a context of sexual education and discussion about relationships. It can be of no real help to the pupil unless it has a locus in life and not just in the laboratory.

It is, under the Education Act 1993, a matter for governors of schools what should be taught in sex education. The law was constructed in this way to allow each school to reflect the wishes of its parents and its community. There was fear that there had been too liberal an attitude adopted towards sexual matters in schools and that there should be a retrenchment and a reaffirmation of traditional sexual and moral values. Some argued that teachers could not be trusted to provide this and so it is a matter for the governors of individual schools to decide if sex education is to be taught at all. How it is taught *is* a matter for teachers nevertheless. Sex education cannot be an isolated subject which stands on its own otherwise it becomes simply a matter of sexual mechanics: human biology under another title. If it is to have an impact on behaviour as well as on knowledge, it must acknowledge the starting point of its pupils as social beings, living in a particular environment, encompassed with mores which may not be those of the teacher. That is not to say that it should not show a better way when necessary, but it cannot begin to do any of these things unless it is part of a personal and social development programme.

Unfortunately, Personal, Social and Health Education (PSHE) is not a subject on the national curriculum. It often does not command specialist teachers and is sometimes seen as a non-essential entry on the timetable. Yet it ought, in the broad terms of what education is really about, to be a central subject for study. PSHE is, if it is anything at all, an attempt to equip pupils to deal with the complexities of moral and social questions for the rest of their lives. In a sense, PSHE looks at the very difficult 'why?' questions of life and as such is preparing its students to make hard decisions about their own lives and those of the people they meet. It is not training. Rather, it is education in its purest form. PSHE can be said to suffuse the whole life of a school.

Because PSHE deals with matters of relationships, it provides opportunities for pupils to speak, perhaps in guarded terms, about some of the issues identified earlier: bullying and abuse. It also offers chances to look more closely at self-respect, mutual respect and assertiveness. These three topics seem crucial to an effective preventative programme when considering child prostitution.

Whatever form of prostitution, and Donovan (1991) identifies two types of young male prostitute which might usefully be applied to young female prostitution as well – Hard Core or the Enthusiastic Amateur – there appears to be a loss of self-respect in the young people engaged in it. The Hard Core group is described as being made up of young people for whom prostitution is an integral part of a life which may also include drug abuse, theft and robbery. The Enthusiastic Amateur is seen as a young person who only engages in prostitution occasionally to get enough money for a particular reason. The Hard Core group is already outside the norms of society and receives no respect from it. The young people in this group may be seen to have chosen a path which alienates them from the norm, for whatever reason. If they are already isolated from the community, it is inevitable that they will have an underlying view of themselves as failures and worthless (or at best, worth less). Equally, the Enthusiastic Amateur is driven by such a desire for something, which may be as basic as food or lodging, that nothing that can happen to them is too bad if it achieves the goal. This loss of self-esteem, seen so often by EWOs working with non-attending pupils of secondary age, is seriously damaging even if it does not lead inevitably to prostitution by children and young people.

Children who believe that they are, as individuals, important and have something to contribute to the general good are more likely to be able to avoid some of the dramatic dangers of life. In a number of schools there have been successful experiments with self-esteem building groups, sometimes arranged by the school, sometimes by an EWO or youth worker. Those engaged in that work often report that the young people involved have heard only negative messages from school. Their work is not good enough or their behaviour is always being criticised without help to improve it. That their teachers often believe that the work could be better (because the pupil has greater ability than has been shown) or that the behaviour could improve because the pupil has the social skills necessary, does not change the outcome. The teacher thinks that encouragement is being offered. The pupil thinks the criticism is unfair. The communication breakdown leads to a loss of self-respect and self-esteem. In turn, that may lead to unauthorised absence from school and if this loss is reinforced from other sources such as family or acquaintances, young people are quite likely to give up on themselves and begin to believe what they hear.

The restoration of self-esteem in such circumstances is not difficult, provided it has not gone too far. Its early recognition is, therefore, important. A child who no longer sees much of worth in his or her own life may have that overcome through the intervention in a positive and purposeful way by a caring adult. It matters little who the adult is. It could be a teacher, an EWO, a youth worker or any other of the educational professionals engaged to help. It must be someone who provides three things: first, and most importantly, time that is clearly seen as the child's by right. Regular, frequent private time is a key factor. Secondly, the helping adult must offer an ear that hears. That means understanding the child's difficulties and helping devise realistic approaches to them. Thirdly, the child needs a respect that is based on an acceptance of the equality of the adult and the child in that relationship: the adult is not better than the child, just older and with different experience. The latter is sometimes difficult to negotiate in a school setting.

Only when people can respect themselves for what they are will they be in a position to respect other people for what they are. Mutual respect means that a child is operating in a social context. Schools spend a great deal of time encouraging their pupils to work in co-operation with each other. That may take the form of academic work or it may have a more overtly social form through rules about conduct within the premises. If a pupil has learned to recognise in others their own worth, no matter how different they may be, it becomes harder to adopt the predatory attitude shown by some young people engaged in prostitution towards their punters. As well as the usual school activities, in and out of the classroom, which encourage mutual respect, there have been a number of projects designed to foster it directly. Outward Bound activities are often cited as examples. They are, though, not the only ones where young people can learn to work co-operatively and to value the contribution made by all. Disaffected older secondary pupils have been seen to benefit from placements in primary schools as classroom assistants. They have learned to work with (rather than against) teachers and with children who look to them for leadership. Work experience placements in which the achievement of the task depends upon joint effort, particularly if undertaken in conjunction with improving self-esteem, have been shown to be helpful.

Nevertheless, despite the positive attempts schools and the whole of the education system may employ to help children and young people develop into fulfilled, confident and assertive adults, we are faced with the knowledge that some young people are today engaged in prostituting themselves for a variety of reasons. A disproportionate number of them have been, or in theory are, in the care of the local authority (Lee and O'Brien, 1995). It has long been recognised that the education of children in care has produced less than satisfactory results (Jackson, 1983; Kahan, 1985). While this is not entirely the responsibility of the educational services – for as Essen *et al.* showed so long ago (1976), children are in care because they have problems which are often unconnected with education – there is no doubt that schools can play a significant part in addressing their needs.

All children need success and security. This is even more so for children in care. Their lives are often catalogues of failure, real or imagined, and of movement from temporary home to temporary home. Schools can offer the stability and opportunity for success that such children need. Co-operation between social workers and teachers is vital to the achievement of these goals. Care needs to be taken to maintain regularity of education when changes in placement are unavoidable. Children in care need to be certain that there is an understanding that they have problems which are beyond the school's competence, but which are recognised by the school as very influential. The staff of residential units and foster parents need to show their support for education as an improving and valuable experience. Above all, teachers and social workers need to be seen to be working together, and jointly with the child, to capitalise on abilities and to be realistic in their expectations.

Low achievement in school results in poor qualifications, which reduce chances of satisfying employment prospects, which tends to lead to low income. That cycle is bad enough for the school leaver who has a stable and supportive home from which to operate. For the care leaver, who may have little help and be expected to be much more self-sufficient than most people of that age, the pattern can be destructive.

Low self-esteem, low achievement and low levels of transitory support when coming together must indicate the likelihood of poor future experience. It is hardly surprising that the basic need for money in such circumstances can drive young people into prostitution. All this is hard for schools to overcome for they are institutions designed to meet the needs of the generality of pupils and find it difficult to fit themselves around the needs of the individual pupil. This is especially problematic when it comes to the reintegration into class of a pupil who has run away and maintained her-/himself in prostitution. The pupil's experiences, self-image and lifestyle will be different from those of the others in the class. They will be radically different from those of the teachers. That needs to be acknowledged from the beginning. However, that does not imply that teachers must abandon their own beliefs and moral code. What they must learn to do is differentiate between the child's behaviour and the child as a person. The fault, the guilt, is not the child's and must always be seen as belonging to the adults who took advantage of the circumstances which the child was in. The return of a child is not the time for reproach but for renewing efforts and making a fresh start for everyone involved. The model of the parable of the Prodigal Son must not be overlooked. Extra help may be needed, and this may cause complaints about depriving others who have avoided such misfortune, but it should be provided in a caring and humane community.

There may be need for counselling, which is not the answer to all problems, or for additional teaching help when work has got behind and success appears to be unachievable. If those things are wanted, they should be available even in times of economic stringency. There should be a concerted plan of activity. Young people who have been engaged in prostitution have, it should be remembered, been robbed of their childhood by adults seeking their own gratification. That applies as much to those who prostitute themselves for extra cash as it does to those who sell themselves to stay alive or are forced into it by their family or carers. Such children should be active partners in the plans that are being made for them, not simply subject to the beneficence of others. As Donovan (1991) records in his sketch of 'Barry', this rent boy's particular skill was in his 'ability to handle any person in authority, in any given situation ... In this he was adept and adroit. This is perhaps the trademark of the successful rent boy – the skills of a survivor!' To attempt to impose, even with the best motives, a regime over such a young person is to ignore their experience and background.

None of this is easy for those involved in education. The problem has barely been recognised. We would prefer it not to be there. But it is a real issue for pupils in cities, towns and rural communities across the country. Schools can make a major contribution to its prevention through their acceptance and careful handling of child protection matters, their thoughtful development of PSHE, and their willingness to provide a secure and caring place for children with problems. They can also do more to combat school exclusions. Schools can offer a fresh start to those who seek it, understanding that children involved in prostitution are coming back into education from an experience that few of us can share but all of us must accept. They can help dispel the prevalent treatment of these children as criminals and see them as the exploited and those who have yet to establish sound human relationships within the mores of our society. In brief, schools and all the other supportive parts of the education system can show that they care about their individual pupils, no matter what these young people's personal histories are.

As Maher (1987) writes to teachers about abused children in general, 'For the sake of those children and the thousands more who will die or suffer in future generations, we need to accept responsibility and take action; and we need that action *now!*'. That fervent sentiment needs translating into the context of child prostitution because schools can and do make a difference.

6. Young People and Prostitution from a Youth Service Perspective

Judith K Green, Sue Mulroy and Maggie O'Neill

Prostitution is commonly defined as an activity where sexual acts are exchanged for payment. However, payment need not be a monetary transaction but could be a place to stay, something to eat, drugs or other payment in kind. Indeed a young person's introduction to prostitution may occur when he or she is without basic necessities and continuing involvement results when these needs are not met from elsewhere. Research has shown that for many children and young people on the street, prostitution is a survival activity sometimes used in addition to theft and begging. (LEE AND O'BRIEN, 1995)

Our experiences and the available literature tell us that there is a huge gap in service provision to young women and to young men involved in prostitution (Barrett, 1995). To this end, we focus upon the necessary interrelation between youth service provision and health service provision in developing a model which pivots around the central involvement of the youth service in responding to the needs of young people involved, or at risk of involvement, in prostitution. Within this paper we use the broad term 'youth service' to describe the personal and social education of young people which takes place within the maintained sector, the traditional voluntary sector and the independent sector. Our central point and recommendation in this chapter is to present the youth service as the integral lynch pin or a central pivot in the development of multi-agency working and multi-agency outcomes with and for young people working in prostitution. In our professional capacities we have all worked mostly with young women but we are, of course, also concerned with young men involved in prostitution. In the following sections we build up a picture of our model. We specifically address the interrelationship of the youth service and the health service in meeting the needs of these young people. To begin with, we articulate the statutory frameworks that inform both the work of the youth service and the work of the health service within the context of the current socio-legal situation. We then move on to delineate our recommendations along multi-agency lines.

THE CONTEXT OF THE CURRENT SITUATION

The removal of benefits for 16- and 17-year-olds, the introduction of lower benefit rates for under 25-year-olds, the introduction of the Housing Act in March 1989 and changes to arrangements for hostel payments towards the end of 1989 had the overall impact of impoverishing further many already impoverished and vulnerable young people. Add to this reduced youth training, low wages, lack of affordable housing and the introduction of the community charge in April 1990, and it is hardly surprising that frontline youth workers across the country noticed an increase in the numbers of young people selling sex in order to survive (Green, 1992). Green argues that practitioners exposed a clear link between the social, economic and personal experiences of young women and homelessness. However, at this time many services addressing young people's housing needs were directed at young men. In many areas emergency accommodation for young women, and specifically young women with children, was rare, if available at all. In 1991, Shelter identified that there were far fewer hostel places for women than men: nationally, there were nine times as many places available for men as women (Dibblin, 1991). Dibblin states: 'Young women are among the most hidden and unrecognised of all homeless people ... their level of invisibility is matched only by their suffering' (1991).

Since the publication of *It's No Game* (Green, 1992) we have experienced the introduction of the Child Support Agency. The CSA has been criticised for: targeting working-class families with already limited financial resources; penalising or threatening women with a reduction or withdrawal of their benefits if they refuse to name the father of their children; and for 'forcing' women to remain in contact with violent partners/fathers. We have also witnessed the introduction of age-related housing benefits, with reductions to single young people under 25 years of age and a general driving down of benefits including: restricted housing benefit for private tenants; the total withdrawal of benefits from most people seeking asylum; and the payment of housing benefit in arrears for all claimants except council tenants. In addition, the government's new Housing Act of 1996 will:

- limit the help available to people accepted as homeless by local authorities;

- promote the use of expensive private renting for homeless households, the majority of whom have low incomes;

- make it easier for private landlords to evict people in rent arrears.

Shelter, the national campaign for homeless people, expects these social security cuts to result in increased homelessness and warns of a substantial rise in the number of people sleeping rough (see Shelter briefing 'How four new benefit rules will increase homelessness in 1996'). A recent research report *Discounted Voices: Homelessness amongst Young Black and Minority Ethnic People in England* (Davies *et al.*, 1996) has found that young single homeless people from black and ethnic minority communities are increasing disproportionately to their numbers in the total population. There is evidence that this is linked directly to racial disadvantage, particularly differentials in unemployment rates, overcrowding and housing conditions, breakdown in personal relations within households, sexual violence, leaving care, leaving penal institutions and eviction from insecure accommodation. Furthermore, white homeless young people are more likely than their black counterparts to use statutory and voluntary agencies for assistance (Children's Legal Centre, 1996a). Both the government and certain sections of the media have further stigmatised young single mothers in particular, with ongoing debates about their status as 'deserving' or 'undeserving' poor and in suggesting a link between teenage pregnancies and housing allocation.

A decade ago, we rarely saw young homeless people begging or sleeping on the streets but this is now a commonplace sight in many towns and cities, even rural areas. We avert our eyes in order to avoid thinking about how this could be, rather than acknowledging that some of the nation's most vulnerable children and young people are being denied access to basic civil rights and services which should be addressing their needs as a matter of paramount importance. Many of these children and young people become caught up in subcultures, and milieux including the criminal justice system, which first institutionalises and then perpetuates the process of criminalisation.

In the areas within which we work we are consequently witnessing an increase in the numbers of girls and young women, including single parents, entering prostitution as a viable alternative to low or no wages and/or having escaped broken families, residential care, homelessness, sexual, physical, emotional abuse or neglect – a national picture is not available. Many of these girls and young women enter prostitution and run with all the associated risks in order to *survive* as they are denied an adequate income by any other means.

THE STATUTORY FRAMEWORKS THAT INFORM THE SPECIALISMS OF THE YOUTH SERVICE AND HEALTH SERVICE

The youth service operates without an explicit statutory base, though it is shaped by the 1944 Education Act as revised by the 1988–92 education legislation, and is part of local authority statutory responsibility for further education. In practice, it operates through partnerships between local authority provision and a whole raft of voluntary and independent groups and organisations, some of which operate at local, regional, national and international levels. Whilst the philosophy of the service is essentially educational, not all local youth services are based within education departments. As a consequence of local government reorganisations and education cuts, many youth services now find themselves within, for example, leisure, community education, or play and recreation departments. For example, Nottinghamshire Youth Service is based within the Leisure Services Department; Wolverhampton within Community, Play and Youth; and Northampton within Education and Libraries. Ironically, it is often some of these services that have best survived the devastating cuts which have virtually destroyed some other education-based services whilst maintaining a distinct youth work philosophy.

The lack of a statutory base has both advantages and disadvantages. It has offered youth workers a level of flexibility within their work and often enabled them to find their own niche, to look for gaps in local services and to set up provision to meet young people's needs where not already provided. It enables workers to lobby, campaign and act as advocates on behalf of young people. Youth work then is largely concerned with the informal social education of young people, both within group work situations and on an individual basis. The work can take place in a variety of young people's settings including: lunch-time clubs in schools and community colleges; local authority youth clubs and centres; through outreach work; detached work projects; girls' and young women's groups; sports and leisure centres; young people's drop-in centres; young people's advice, information and counselling services or through mobile projects; as well as the most instantly and publicly recognised organisations such as the Scouts, the Guides, arts-based organisations, or sports or activity centred groups.

An important recent development is the way in which youth work skills and approaches are increasingly being recognised and adopted by other organisations and service providers. Youth workers are increasingly being employed by health authorities and trusts, for example, in order to develop creative ways of working with young people. Outreach and detached work, drop in, information and advice centres and peer education approaches are all now in use in order to move towards attaining the Health of the Nation targets (Department of Health, 1991) in relation to sexual health and young people. Many health services now work closely with the youth service in order to reach marginalised or disenfranchised young people who may not have access to existing services. The health service has looked to the youth service for models of good practice in terms of philosophies of empowerment and appropriate methods of working with young people. Where adequate funding exists, particularly innovative work has developed. Problematically, the intended removal of ring-fenced HIV/AIDS monies from the end of March 1997 by the Department of Health for treatment and cure, but most importantly in relation to prevention, could have a major impact upon both existing work and future developments.

Whilst this list of settings in which youth work takes place is not exhaustive, the commonality is that young people become involved in the youth service on a voluntary basis. In other words they 'vote with their feet'. They participate because they want to rather than being required to as with, for example, formal education, social or probation services. There is no imposed obligation placed upon them, which makes the relationship that exists between youth workers and young people unique.

The key youth work approaches now being adopted and fostered by health promotion and education workers are: a holistic approach; peer education; harm minimisation or risk reduction; preventative work; and crisis intervention. We will elaborate a little on each of these in turn.

A *holistic approach* means working with the 'whole' person. In working with young people this means recognising that the issues which affect young people's lives are not separate but necessarily interrelated. For example, work with young prostitutes funded through HIV/AIDS monies acknowledges that HIV needs to be addressed within the overall context of the young person's life. One helpful approach, for example, is to counsel and refer young women to services best suited to meet the individual's differing needs as well as offering a drop-in facility off street and outreach sessions on street. Trust, confidentiality and a genuine concern and care for the person as a whole are crucial to the dynamics operating between the helping professional and the young woman/ women he or she works with. A holistic approach within this context is best met through effective inter-agency collaboration.

Peer education is about training and supporting young people to work with other young people around specific issues of concern to them. It is a working process which aims to develop knowledge, attitudes and skills as well as confidence and self-esteem in order for young people to make informed choices about their own behaviour, beliefs and attitudes. There is an increasing number of peer education projects established between health and youth services. The Leicestershire Health Promotion Centre, for example, employs health promotion officers who are trained youth workers to co-ordinate, deliver and support a peer education project which trains young women to become sexual health peer educators and then work with young people in informal and formal settings. Further to this, the Leicester based WHIP project (Women's Health in Prostitution) based within Leicestershire AIDS Support Services (LASS) has recently employed a trained youth worker to develop peer education approaches to work with prostitutes, with young women at risk, particularly within the student population and with young women leaving care.

Harm minimisation or *risk reduction* recognises that children and young people are sometimes pressurised to take risks and that there are many factors which influence risk-taking behaviours beyond lack of knowledge. This approach therefore takes practical action to reduce risks by, for example, distributing condoms/femidoms to young people in order to encourage safer sexual practices. It also involves the provision of appropriate advice and information which is relevant and acknowledges the lifestyles of the young people it aims to reach.

Preventative work involves adopting and implementing strategies for prevention and attempts to discourage young people from taking risks. Youth workers and other educationalists act as role models/mentors and, given trusting relationships, they are in positions to address some of the issues associated with risk-taking and the negative outcomes, for example, aspects connected with birth control.

Crisis intervention involves intervening when young people are in crisis situations, such as living on the street, homeless, involved in drug cultures, street cultures and/or prostitution. Offering a holistic approach to young people in this situation is critical in order to try and address the most pressing immediate needs (which might be for shelter or for food) whilst also working through peer education and/or harm minimisation to prevent further harm, getting the young person to a place of safety; and/or to try and develop relationships of trust and confidentiality so that welfare and health needs can be met and the skills, confidence or resources developed to lead a different lifestyle.

The future of the youth service and the way it might be delivered may be unclear, particularly with regard to local government reorganisations, but there is no doubt that youth workers are in a unique position to support young women and other young people both on and off street. What is evident is that youth workers can often do this more effectively than other workers from the statutory services, particularly as some of these young people will already have had negative experiences of statutory services. Youth workers, working alongside other key services, are in a unique position to befriend, support and advocate on behalf of the young people involved. It is absolutely vital, however, that this work is underpinned by supportive policies, inter-agency collaboration and up-to-date training for staff.

Unlike the youth service, the health service operates within a statutory framework. This includes attempts to reduce the incidence of HIV and other STDs in various 'target groups' via a harm minimisation process. This process aims to inform, educate, empower and enable members of the 'target group' to make informed decisions and choices about their sexual health needs. Within this framework, health workers aim to address and develop the health promotion ideology, attitude, knowledge and skills of 'clients' in order to reduce the incidence of HIV and other STDs. It is therefore implicit within this framework to approach health from a holistic perspective.

Recent guidelines from the Department of Health (1996) indicate that female sex workers are no longer seen as in need of direct HIV resource funding (i.e. there is no legal requirement). These guidelines can be interpreted on a local level depending upon the needs identified in local HIV strategies. In one locality the guidelines have been interpreted to allow for developing a project to address the needs of 'sex workers' and 'vulnerable young women'. However, in areas where the guidelines are not interpreted to enable the continuation and development of such services, a reduced amount of direct health work being carried out from outreach services may ensue.

The health service has demonstrated a commitment to working with marginalised young women by commissioning projects around the country where the empowerment of these women is of fundamental importance. The health service acknowledges that the health of women is an issue that needs to be maintained within a holistic approach to the overall wellbeing of women. In order to continue to build upon existing good practice and develop new initiatives, youth services and health services must continue to develop and build on current links in order to meet the needs of vulnerable and marginalised groups of young people.

One of the authors has been informed by identifying models of good practice from other sex worker projects in Britain, for example, the work of POW! (Prostitute Outreach Workers, based in Nottingham), WHIP (Women's Health in Prostitution, based in Leicester) and the SAFE project based in Birmingham, one of the earliest and most pioneering of projects in this country to identify and meet the needs of hundreds of women involved in prostitution. Due to the innovative method of outreach HIV prevention work commissioned by her health authority, she is able to bring a youth work ideology into her current practice. The project aims to enable prostitutes to make autonomous decisions about their wellbeing by building trusting working relationships with the women concerned. In taking this approach, the project is then able to work with women in addressing what they define as their priority needs.

The main issues that arise from the experiences of outreach projects working with women and young people working as prostitutes are summarised as follows:

i) *In situ* HIV and sexual health work is not generally a major priority for female sex workers who often have many other multiple needs that take priority, such as homelessness, violence, drugs and poverty.

ii) Research does indicate that most prostitutes are at risk of HIV via incidents of sexual violence or abuse rather than unprotected sex in negotiated interactions. (Kinnell, 1992).

iii) The criminalisation of female prostitutes tends to perpetuate the need for young women to continue working in order to pay fines.

iv) Policing policies and actions can hinder developing relationships between outreach workers and sex workers if the role of the outreach worker is not understood. High profile policing also puts the female sex worker at more risk of violence as it can serve to displace women from areas they know well to areas they are unsure of and/or push sex work further underground.

v) Options or exit strategies are often not apparent to women/young people or to outreach workers. Linking into local youth service provision could enable a more proactive approach by the outreach worker to support and facilitate options for women/young people wishing to exit prostitution.

vi) The further problem facing workers in undertaking street-based work with prostitutes is the need for female sex workers to engage their clients on the street. This creates problems around the timing of contact with each woman and of resident backlashes towards prostitutes, which are becoming more common. Pimps may also reject the outreach workers' interventions on behalf of the women.

These difficulties all inhibit the development of deeper working relationships with young people involved in prostitution. Youth services operating in tandem with health outreach workers and supported by police services, probation services, magistrates, mental health services, educationalists and social services could provide a model which offers a better organised network of services to young people; the possibility of developing options or exit routes for these young people and developing preventative work with young people in local authority care could also be considered. Local Area Child Protection Committees (ACPCs) could play an important lead role here in initiating a youth service response with children they think are 'at risk'.

Certainly, for the work one of the authors is involved in, multi-agency work has broadened the range of *in situ* service provision such as needle exchange and drug harm minimisation programmes, as the project works closely with the local Drug Link project. Personal safety is highlighted both on and off street by distributing resources such as mug sheets (information sheets stating dates, times and identifying features) of 'dodgy punters' (clients who have robbed/raped/attacked or assaulted women working on or off street), personal attack alarms and information on keeping safe.

A continuity of relationships has evolved between the outreach workers and female prostitutes. Many of the women have not previously been able to maintain long-term relationships due to the nature of their lives. For instance, if they are from backgrounds of being in local authority care, many will have experienced several moves between residential units and/or foster families. Also, if they are pimped, then they are often moved around between differing locales. Developing trusting relationships, relationships which bring continuity, is a vital aspect of work with alienated, marginalised and criminalised young people.

We have experience of one health authority that has taken the lead in addressing some of the needs of young female sex workers. However, a single agency alone cannot address and develop interventionary strategies to meet the overall needs of women and young people involved in prostitution, needs which stem from specific psycho-social and socio-economic factors. A multi-agency response led from a youth service perspective *or* a joint health and youth service led approach based on the principles of a youth service is, we feel, a positive and purposeful way forward in dealing with the complexities involved in working with children, young people and women involved in prostitution.

MULTI-AGENCY POSSIBILITIES AND THE ROLE OF THE YOUTH SERVICE

We argue that the youth service should be integral in liaising, raising awareness and meeting the training needs/development needs of a range of statutory organisations. In turn, it is important for these services to adopt a youth work philosophy or youth work approaches to their own interventions and work with young people. An important dimension we raise here is the vital link between youth work and health work. In many locations the health service has begun to adapt and adopt youth service approaches in an attempt to address attitudes/knowledge and behaviour of young people. Health authorities have looked to the youth service for models of good practice in terms of philosophies of empowerment and approaches such as peer education, outreach and detached work. Possibilities for multi-agency working which pivot around the work and approach of the youth service need to be contextualised within the current legal, social and political frameworks in order to better understand the necessary interrelation between agencies working with and for young people. In turn, this will enable us to develop more informed responses and interventionary strategies around child/juvenile prostitution along multi-agency lines.

In *The Game's Up: Redefining Child Prostitution*, Lee and O'Brien (1995) give us a thorough and comprehensive account of child prostitution in current British society, focusing specifically upon street prostitution. The report focuses upon children and young people under the age of 18 years. It concerns itself largely with the legal framework of child protection and prostitution and also the legal responses to child prostitution. The report concludes that there *is* a legal framework in place for responding to the needs of children and young people involved in prostitution. Lee and O'Brien point out that the Children Act 'provides for the development of services to young people in need and many young people involved in prostitution will have a series of needs that are not being met' (1995). Further to this, the Act also provides 'for inter-agency work on child protection and emergency intervention when the welfare of the child is at risk.'

There is extensive legislation already in place that is used against young people involved in prostitution, for example, Section 12 and Section 32 of the 1956 Sexual Offences Act and Section 1 of the 1959 Street Offences Act. There is also 'a range of punitive measures that can be taken against clients, pimps and other people who may be directly or indirectly involved. This could include hoteliers, club owners and land-lords ... and, if used effectively, could remove the financial incentive for some of those involved in the sexual exploitation of children and young people' (Lee and O'Brien, 1995). In addition to the Acts named above, these potential measures include the Indecency with Children Act 1960, the Sexual Offences Act 1985, the Sexual Offences Act 1967 and the Local Government Miscellaneous Provisions Act 1982.

However, despite the availability of the legislative framework in law and the admirable and desperately needed recommendations from the United Nations and Europe, in British law children can on the one hand be protected from sexual exploitation and abuse and on the other hand, as *The Game's Up* indicates, children as young as ten can be 'prosecuted for offences relating to that abuse'. This revolves (as for women involved in prostitution) around a notion of deserving of intervention or undeserving of intervention. Lee and O'Brien state that in 'criminalising young people, the police – informed by a perception of which young people are "innocent" and deserving of protection and which are not – are simply emphasising one section of legislation over another'. This, they maintain, can lead to a situation where the children of a man known to use child prostitutes would be the subject of investigation whereas the children he uses as prostitutes would not. The report concludes that more emphasis must be placed upon the welfare of young people under the auspices of the Children Act and less use made of the criminal justice system. It is simply inappropriate to deal with children and young people involved in prostitution within the criminal justice system, which is the current situation in Britain.

Rather, we should be working towards the recommendations made by the UN, by the Council of Europe and the European Forum on Child Welfare within the context of operationalising the Children Act. Certainly, the UK sections of the Confederation of Family Organisations in the European Union (COFACE) agreed that there should be special recognition of children in the Treaties of the European Union, arguing that the 'development of children's rights requires the foundation of a European treaty base' (Watt, 1996). Watt argues, and we agree, that 'a new and unequivocal children's rights Article to the Treaties, giving the Commission power to issue Directives, rather than Recommendations, would accomplish this important step'. Realistically, Watt acknowledges that simply getting children's rights onto the European agenda is a small victory and one step further to full recognition.

The development of a youth service perspective which brings together health services and welfare services in multi-agency strategies and initiatives to address both *prevention* of involvement in prostitution and *responses* to involvement in prostitution geared to the emotional, physical and cultural needs of our most vulnerable children and young people is urgently needed. In recent years, the government has been instrumental in rolling back state welfare services at the same time as implementing a strong central controlling state which looks down on the poor and marginalised, thus reinstating an ethos of individualism which focuses the 'blame' on the backs of this group.

Barbara Gibson worked as a health consultant for Streetwise Youth in London, a unique charity targeting and working exclusively with young, male, homeless street prostitutes (known as 'rent boys') and offering a holistic service. She states that most of the young men she has worked with have lacked most of the basic needs children require as defined by the NSPCC: 'love, trust, respect, physical care, attention and praise' (Gibson, 1995). With unhappy childhoods, deprived, neglected, and mistreated, they lack self-confidence and self-worth. These experiences are reflected in our own work with young women and young men involved in selling sex. These common experiences also run through the lives of the young people present in the work of Nicholsen (1981), McMullen (1987), Sereny (1984), West and de Villiers (1992), Ennew (1986), Gibson (1995) and Lee and O'Brien (1995).

Listening to young people reveals the significance of a range of factors and experiences: the effect of pre-care familial experiences; routes into care; peer group pressure and the 'culture of care'; male violence and peer abuse; the feelings expressed by young people of abandonment, hopelessness and the need to 'belong'; experiences of 'doing' crime and 'doing' prostitution (O'Neill, 1996).

Angela:
Care needs changing a lot – a lot ... and people in homes have been abused that much they just turn to work ... out on the street ... when I first started working I said 'oh well, I might as well go out and get paid for working rather than getting abused by someone' ... that's when I first started working ... then I fell into a trap with a bloke ... and I only got out of that last year ... that's how the kids turn out ... they've had a rough life and they get put in care ... and they have a rough life ... they are going to come out and still be the same as when they first went in ... or worse. (O'NEILL *ET AL.*, 1995)

Alice:
I have been abused and all that stuff. I have never had parents who actually cared, never had like lots of money to give me ... and like presents given to me ... do you know what I mean ... when I was two I went into care ... I nearly died because I was so abused ... I stayed in hospital for a year ... when I was fifteen I went into this ... independent flats with staff there ... it's not like a secure unit ... you can go out and do what you want ... but you see I didn't like it ... I didn't want to go there but I was made to go there ... I was attacked there ... not actually attacked ... but you know ... like raped ... I got that ... that happened to me ... another resident he got two years ... he comes out this year ... I had to go through all that ... I had to go to hospital and all that stuff ... I had to have tests ... I felt like I wanted to be dead ... do you know what I mean ... there was nothing there ... do you understand? (O'NEILL, 1996)

Pat:
When I was seventeen and I used to work on the beat ... I was pregnant with my little boy ... and I got in this car and he took me everywhere and he told me 'get in the back '... and he started pulling my hair ... and I just burst into tears and told him I was pregnant ... it was my idea to go out ... we didn't think I could claim until eighteen ... because I was so young ... we didn't think I could get benefit at all. (MULROY AND O'NEILL, 1997)

Pat was put into voluntary care at age 12 following her being sexually abused by an elderly man who lived nearby. Psychiatric help and 'unruly' behaviour together with a mum and stepdad who couldn't 'cope' with her combined to facilitate her entry into local authority care. Pat began to work on street to make money for herself and her boyfriend on leaving care at 16; they were not aware that she could claim money from the Department of Social Security. Alice entered local authority care as a toddler: she had been sexually abused by her father and was hospitalised for a long time as the abuse was so severe. When interviewed she was living independently and attending college but felt a very deep lack of self-confidence and self-doubt. She describes herself as 'surviving'. Angela entered local authority care at the age of two. 'I have been all over—I have been adopted—that broke down—when I was nine—I have been in different foster carers—they wanted me to be someone different—they said "I wish we had you when you were different without these problems" ... I have been in four kid's homes and 13 foster homes' (O'Neill *et al.*, 1995).

By working in multi-agency ways with committed individuals from the various agencies all working both with and for young people, we can together explore, foster and develop change which is gender aware and focuses upon sexuality; racial, sexual and social identity; the interrelation of education, welfare and health needs; the whole spectrum of incivilities that young children and young people face including intimidation, harassment and lack of care, physical, sexual and emotional violence. The list includes lack of support when leaving care, lack of support in the community, lack of continuity of care; and the relationships with courts, police, remand institutions and secure accommodation. We need to develop work which better understands children and young people's experiences and acts upon that understanding. We can aim to achieve this by developing action research projects, by analysing the available literature, by listening to practitioners in projects working with children and young people and then by developing policy-oriented practice in *collaboration* with young people and with the statutory and voluntary agencies working with and for them.

It is vital that we listen to young people and together develop social knowledge as social critique which is then used in a purposeful way to develop policy-oriented practice – social policy initiatives to improve the lived experiences of our children. It may appear a banal truism, but our children are our future.

SUMMARY AND RECOMMENDATIONS

Responding to young people's needs should be our priority. We can find out what their needs are by talking to them, by talking to experienced or appropriate youth workers, educationalists and health workers delivering frontline services to children and young people involved in prostitution. A multi-agency response to young people's needs must mobilise to change the current socio-legal situation so that protection, harm minimisation and the welfare of the children and young people is absolutely paramount.

We have illustrated that the mechanisms are already in place; we simply need to make sure our actions and training of workers involved in the criminal justice process operationalise the recommendations presented by Lee and O'Brien(1995) through the introduction of directives, not recommendations. Indeed, a national organisation that makes recommendations for young people and children would be a welcome addition.

Certainly, more effective targeting of child abusers is vital. Young people and children involved in prostitution must not be criminalised or seen as 'deserving' victims. They are children and young people who suffer at the hands of men who desire, fantasise and buy sex with children – paedophiles. We wonder how the recent tragic death of Daniel, from the east end of London (murdered by two paedophiles), would have been interpreted and dealt with by the media and the criminal justice system had he been working as a child prostitute. The youngest boy one of us has talked to who was 'working' was nine at the time but had been involved in 'the scene' from eight years of age.

Participatory action research to develop effective interventionary strategies is needed. Multi-agency working groups could form the foundations for support and also the mechanisms for implementing the recommendations of any such research. This research should include the young people at all stages in the process; any outcomes and recommended actions following such research would need to be followed up.

The training of staff/workers in both statutory and voluntary organisations working with children and young people is a priority. The youth service provides an admirable role model for other organisations and agencies in that it is rooted in experiential learning, models of systematic supervision and in peer support and development.

Resources and commitment are needed to develop and foster multi-agency working from a youth service perspective. Ring-fenced funding is still possible in the current climate, given an explicit commitment to address the issues as outlined. We cannot afford to simply turn over the page, walk away, or sigh in disbelief at the experiences and needs of these young people. They are our most vulnerable children. The way we choose to address and act on this issue is a marker of our humanism as a society, or our barbarism.

The common link between all three of us, the authors, is a commitment to multi-agency working, a concern with and for young people involved in prostitution and a desperate need to involve ourselves in both the debate and policy-oriented action by making recommendations on the basis of our own work and experiences with and for children and young people.

7. Positive Awareness: Health Professionals' Response to Child Prostitution

Jean Faugier and Mary Sargeant

Investigating and understanding the behaviour of prostitutes has, until recently, been an under-researched area in the UK. In the 1980s, the advent of the AIDS virus brought about an increase in research on adult prostitutes (particularly females) and their risk behaviour patterns. However, published work concerning juvenile prostitution remains scarce and tends to focus on family alienation and child abuse (O'Neill *et al.*, 1995). Although there has been media interest surrounding sex tourism, child pornography and paedophile sex rings (Joseph, 1995), the life experience of the young people concerned continues to remain unclear and this, in turn, hampers our ability to make meaningful responses to their situation.

In addition, apart from the role played by health care professionals in the field of child protection, the benefits of utilising their skills in the assessment and management of children at risk have also remained under researched. Health professionals need to understand the contributing factors to child prostitution and be aware of appropriate health promotion initiatives and harm reduction strategies in order to create an awareness of their own professional potential. They need to recognise the cyclic drift through social and situational factors of family breakdown, rejection and deviant behaviour, as described by Jesson (1993), which leaves these children vulnerable to abuse, exploitation and ill health. Influenced by personal characteristics such as depression and anxiety, as well as the family background dynamics of sexuality, poverty, physical and mental abuse and neglect (Jesson, 1993), young prostitutes are at extreme risk and health professionals need to acknowledge that they are in a prime position to intervene with health promotion and coping strategies.

This chapter discusses the contribution that health professionals might make to intervening in the 'careers' of children and young people either at risk of, or involved in, prostitution, and describes some practical health care initiatives which have been set up to help and protect these children. It explores the associated issues of child abuse and neglect, poverty and homelessness, drug abuse, mental and physical health, and the role of health care professionals working within multidisciplinary teams. Descriptive quotes from Faugier's (1996) study of prostitutes, HIV and drugs are used to enrich the contextual understanding of the lives of young prostitutes. Commissioned by the Department of Health, Faugier's study focused on the sexual and drug-related risk behaviour of 100 drug-using prostitutes and 50 non-using prostitutes, all female, and their clients in Manchester.

EARLY LIFE EVENTS – ABUSE AND DEPRIVATION

Research on the long-term mental health consequences of child abuse victims has demonstrated that such abuse impacts negatively on self-esteem and contributes to depression, suicidal feelings and behaviour, and poor mental health (Bagley, 1991). Silverman *et al.* (1996) demonstrate the substantial risk run by abused children and adolescents of developing clinical levels of emotional-behavioural problems and psychiatric disorders, experiencing suicidal thoughts and attempting suicide in later life. They also highlight alarming rates of psychopathology and co-occuring disorders among physically and sexually abused adults at age 21. These findings underscore the need for early intervention and prevention strategies by health professionals, including health visitors and community nurses as well as those working in primary and secondary care, in order to forestall or minimise the serious consequences of child abuse.

The fact that there is a clear connection between juvenile prostitution and a previous history of sexual abuse (Silbert and Pines, 1981; Widom and Ames, 1994) reinforces the need for intervention by child protection and other health care workers. However, it is essential that any such intervention is based on a very real understanding of the issues, a very frank examination of the worker's own sexual feelings with the help of supervision, and a real foundation of skill in working with such emotional issues in depth. As McMullen (1987) points out, child abuse is based on an abuse of power by adults who are frequently those closest to the child. Research in San Francisco by Silbert and Pines (1981) found that, of a sample of children being cared for in a project established to help abuse victims, 33% had been abused by their natural fathers, 67% by a father figure and only 10% by a stranger. In 82% of cases, force was used on the child. According to McMullen (1987), professionals have a responsibility to clearly understand the extent of that abuse of power and to recognise the fact that they may unwittingly continue this abuse by requiring detailed descriptive accounts of the acts of abuse rather than assisting the child or young person to move from the victim state by establishing a trusting relationship in order to help the child deal effectively with the frequently aroused feelings of guilt, responsibility and shame for the abuse. As McMullen states, 'Children do not choose freely to become prostitutes and we must not expect them to simply choose to stop being prostitutes'.

The motivation for prostitution behaviour is extremely complex, even though it is frequently expressed in very simple terms. Young female respondents to Faugier's (1996) study often cited the ease of obtaining high financial rewards, the need to feed a drug habit, or the fact that they were taking the punters for a ride. However, almost all 150 respondents to the survey revealed a history of child abuse at some stage during the interview, even though questions about it were not asked directly. Behind the necessary bravado to continue the life they are involved in, many of these young women were all too painfully struggling to come to terms with a very damaging past which had left them feeling worthless enough to continue their victimisation via prostitution.

CHILD RUNAWAYS

Research has highlighted the link between children's history of sexual abuse and their running away and travelling to large cities, becoming, in most cases, homeless in the process. The risk factors associated with youth homelessness have been found to include: physical and mental illness; anxiety and depression; substance abuse; crime; loss of self-esteem; and loneliness (Children's Legal Centre, 1996b). Running away from home and residential care has been linked with involvement in prostitution (Sereny, 1984; Finkelhor, 1986; Seng, 1989; Pitts, 1992). In particular, homeless young females are more likely to become involved in prostitution, to have been depressed or to have attempted suicide (McCarthy and Hagan, 1992). *Running – the Risk*, a research study carried out by The Children's Society (Stein *et al.*, 1994), describes how young runaways often turn to survival strategies such as crime and prostitution, with at least one in seven having traded sex for money and over a quarter having been physically and/or sexually assaulted whilst on the streets. Many had also indulged in self-harm and suicide attempts.

Lonely, damaged, needy young people and children are an easy target for those adults who wish to exploit or harm them. Denis Neilsen, who abused and murdered young men after taking them back to his London flat, deliberately targeted a well-known London pub as the location to pick up boys who had for whatever reason lost touch with, or run away from, home. Similarly, many of the victims of Rosemary and Fred West were young people with a disrupted or deprived family background. Investigations into these very high profile cases and, more importantly, inquiries surrounding the lives of other children and young people who may end up on the streets or involved in the sex industry, frequently reveal a disturbing lack of communication and liaison between health care, social welfare and criminal justice agencies, all of which at some stage come into contact with such young people. These young people may present in a very angry and aggressive manner at various agencies demanding a bed, money, health care, etc. If professionals respond defensively to this anger rather than attempt to go beyond it and connect with what is frequently intense anxiety and a desire to be helped, they will be viewed as judgemental and moralistic, which will prevent them from achieving any measure of success. Such attitudes only serve to further alienate children and young people at risk by reinforcing the feelings of worthlessness with which they often justify their prostitution activities (Miller, 1995).

THE SUBSTANCE ABUSE CONNECTION

Society is becoming increasingly aware of the growing numbers of young people experimenting with alcohol and illicit drugs. A recent survey by Edinburgh University, published in the *British Medical Journal*, found that in the last seven years there has been a huge rise in the use of soft and hard drugs, alcohol and cigarettes by 15- and 16-year-olds. In fact, nearly half of all 15- to 16-year-olds were found to have tried illegal drugs (*The Guardian*, 17 August, 1996). Young people have been targeted as a potentially vulnerable population for the spread of HIV and evidence suggests that they often combine alcohol and sex (Plant and Foster, 1991). They are also more likely than older people to say that emotions, especially romance and stimulation, influence their drinking habits (Klein and Pittman, 1993).

The relationship between illicit drugs and prostitution has been well documented. In a review of the subject, Goldstein (1979) suggested that between 30% and 70% of female drug users were also prostitutes and that between 40% and 85% of prostitutes were also drug users. More recent studies in the United States, London and Scotland have reported similar findings (Morgan Thomas *et al.*, 1990; McKeganey *et al.*, 1990; Des Jarlais and Friedman, 1987; Gossop *et al.*, 1994). In his study of adolescent prostitution, Weisberg (1985) concluded that: 'Drug use is common among adolescent prostitutes, and few can say they never use drugs. A considerable number have drug problems. Estimates of juvenile prostitutes who use drugs at work range from about one-fifth to two-thirds'. Prostitution is used by some young people as a way of funding their own and their partner's drug habit (Cameron *et al.*, 1993). More at risk from physical and mental abuse, mental illness and sexually transmitted diseases (STDs) – including HIV and AIDS – than their non drug-using counterparts, these young people are an extremely vulnerable group who require skilled intervention work by health professionals. However, although there is frequent contact between young people and health workers for reasons unconnected with prostitution, the link between a drug habit and the means by which many boys and girls on the streets manage to pay for it often remains poorly understood by those professionals, who thus miss a whole number of chances to get these young people to talk about their prostitution (Faugier, 1996).

Apart from substance abuse by the children and adolescents themselves, other factors have proved influential in their career trajectory into prostitution. A number of studies have demonstrated the importance of substance misuse in the home as a predictive factor in child abuse and subsequent involvement in both substance abuse and prostitution (Sheridan, 1995). Greater awareness of substance abuse problems in families and an increased ability on the part of professionals to work with such families could have a significant impact on the early lives of a great many children. Primary health care professionals and other non-specialist health care workers are essential to the process of early detection and intervention which has been known for some time to be highly effective in breaking the cycle of abuse in a number of families (*Report of the Task Force to Review Services for Drug Misusers*, Department of Health, 1996a). However, there is an urgent need to address the skills deficit which many professionals demonstrate in this field. The English National Board for Nursing has recognised the need to improve the skills of nurses, health visitors and midwives in relation to this topic and has recently launched a teaching pack and curriculum guidelines to assist colleges of nursing and nurse tutors. Nurses, health visitors and midwives are often in a unique position in relation to families and, with the appropriate skills, can effectively intervene in problems which impinge very negatively on children. In addition, the recent Health Advisory Service thematic review *Children and Young People: Substance Misuse Services* clearly acknowledges the need to provide comprehensive services for children and young people which cover the whole gamut of health professional activity from simple health promotion to intensive specialist rehabilitation services (NHS Health Advisory Service, 1996).

THE HIV DIMENSION

The emergence of AIDS as a global threat has served to highlight the need for health promotion initiatives aimed at those perceived to be most at risk from contracting and/or transmitting the virus. Between August 1991 and September 1993, the number of AIDS cases among young people aged between 13 to 24 has risen from 8441 to 14,127 (Centres for Disease Control, 1991; 1993). Thousands more are thought to be infected and millions more are at risk (Heinz, 1992). Juvenile prostitutes are also at greater risk from a wide variety of medical problems and health-compromising behaviours, including drug abuse, suicide and depression (Yates *et al.*, 1991). The high level of multiple drug abuse, the greater likelihood of gay or bisexual involvement and the high number of sexual partners means that these young people run a much greater risk of contracting and transmitting HIV. Health professionals with both harm reduction and pre- and post-HIV counselling skills and knowledge are needed to advise this growing group of young people. The recent tragic murder of a young female prostitute in the Midlands (*The Guardian*, 21 August, 1996) demonstrates that children and young people often get involved in prostitution and drugs whilst still attending school. Health professionals and teachers faced with problem school children or dealing with truancy need to be aware of the increased risk of such activities; they also require the skill of asking the right questions in the framework of a supportive relationship.

STATUTORY FRAMEWORK AROUND CHILD ABUSE THAT INFORMS PRACTICE RESPONSE

Following the implementation of the Children Act 1989 and a revised government guidance on child protection, *Working Together under the*

Children Act 1989 (Department of Health *et al.*, 1991), a comprehensive statutory mechanism and legal framework in child protection now exists for nurses, midwives and health visitors. These guidelines emphasise the need for communication and co-operation between professionals and agencies working in the child protection field and stress the importance of specialist education, effective co-ordination, supervision and support for health professionals. In essence, they aim to help prevent professionals working in child protection avoid some of the tragic and widely published errors highlighted in recent child death inquiries.

Health authorities and local authorities must now have an agreed policy on the management of child abuse and child sexual abuse. In each local authority, members of the family health services authority and the health authority/board (including nursing, midwifery, medical and psychiatric representation) are required to be part of an Area Child Protection Committee (ACPC) in conjunction with those from social services departments, the local NSPCC, the police, the probation service and the education service. The ACPC must produce guidelines on the procedures to be followed by nurses, midwives and health visitors working with children at risk of suspected or actual abuse, which are easily accessible by staff and include details of steps to be taken by all those working with children and families. In addition, health authorities/ boards and their staff have a duty to co-operate in child protection actions and activities and must each appoint and identify a named person, often a senior nurse or GP, to co-ordinate child protection work and advise contractors. A senior health professional must also be nominated by the district health authority/board to ensure that child protection policies are in place throughout all provider units within each district.

However, although this system is comprehensive and generally works well, problems do occur. Following the NHS and Community Care Act 1990, serious disruption to communication and support lines has been experienced between managers and professionals within the health services involved in identifying and protecting children at risk. Social services departments have become under pressure and overstretched following the new changes, which they face in addition to the demands of the Children Act. This has meant that 'child protection' and 'children in the community' are now both competing for resources and as a consequence, there are fewer social workers in child protection. This has lead to inter-agency conflicts within the child protection field, most notably, tensions between social workers and health visitors during the referral process (Appleton, 1996; Taylor and Tilley, 1989). A prioritisation process introduced by social workers, where they do not pick up every referral has meant that health visitors are often the sole professional group available to offer assistance both in terms of health and social problems. Health visitors are frustrated by the lack of social services input and aware of the need to document their cases well, with written referrals to social services and diligent follow up.

These role conflicts raise implications for the management and practice of health visiting, with concerns being expressed about the future of health visiting and the underfunding of community nursing services in Britain (Sadler, 1994; Appleton, 1996). A recent survey by the Health Visitors Association (1994) pointed to difficulties faced by health visitors working under stress, often with large caseloads and minimal clinical support from their managers or child protection specialists. It seems that if child protection services are to adapt to these continuing pressures, multi-disciplinary training and support systems, including clinical supervision, need to be introduced and maintained. The importance of training and supervision has also been highlighted in *Child Protection: Messages from Research* (Department of Health, 1995).

PRACTICAL RESPONSE OF HEALTH CARE, INCLUDING HISTORY

Residential care

Research has shown that many drug-using prostitutes have been in care as children, as a prostitute interviewed in Faugier's (1996) study describes.

Mary, aged 33:
I was put in care when I was 8. I've been in every foster home going, family group homes and whatever. When I got to my teenage years, I got really pissed off with it and started to abscond all the time. There was a home at that time in Whalley Range called Alder House; I was in there for 3 years. With being in Whalley Range, when you did a runner, the first place you ran to was Moss Side. When you're an adolescent, you think it's all dead glamorous. I started on the streets at 13, watching out for the older women.

A study by O'Neill *et al.* (1995) on juvenile prostitution and the experience of young women in care emphasises the social stigma and marginalisation attached to being in care. O'Neill stresses the need for interventionary strategies based on young people's requirements as well as for proper training of care staff, and describes the benefits of peer education programmes for young female prostitutes. Also implicit here is that local authorities are generally not fulfilling their responsibility under the 1989 Children Act to support care leavers.

The period of time spent in residential care can provide the opportunity for valuable preventive work, educational advice and information in preparation for leaving care, especially in such areas as risk behaviour, safer drug use, safer sex and contraception. Increased levels of practical and emotional support may be necessary for those leaving care, especially when they have a history of social and emotional deprivation. For many of these young people, a career involving drug use and prostitution may offer too many enticements or may seem the only option available. Emphasis should be placed on assertiveness training, life skills training and social survival, together with information about how to make use of health care.

Empowering young people

Young people's views need to be taken into account when developing services to cater for their needs. Health promotional material written in their language, combined with explanations of what a service has to offer, ease of access and help with wider social issues relating to young people, are important determinants of help-seeking behaviour. Appropriate health education should include information on safer sex techniques, empowering young people to be assertive in their health risk behaviour. It must be acknowledged that some young people are professional prostitutes. Juvenile prostitutes have little, if any, 'apprenticeship' in this respect from older, more knowledgeable prostitutes and generally learn their skills by trial and error. For most juvenile prostitutes, the main worry is not the immediate threat of AIDS, but rather how to get enough money as quickly as possible for drugs whilst avoiding violence, robbery and arrest. Young prostitutes frequently deny the risks they face, in order to survive their encounters with punters.

Although often knowledgeable about AIDS, runaway youths have been found to have few positive attitudes towards prevention (Rotheram-Borus and Koopman, 1991). AIDS prevention programmes are clearly needed to change the beliefs and behaviour of this group, although currently such programmes only seem to produce a short-term reduction in these high-risk behaviours. Slonim-Nevo *et al.* (1996) point out that an explanation for this failure may be that the adolescents concerned do not perceive their future as worth protecting. They argue that knowledge and skills training alone are insufficient to motivate behavioural change, which requires instead a sense of meaning and purpose to be created in these young people's lives. A comprehensive care framework, utilising the skills of educationalists, psychologists and social workers to assist with individual and family counselling, financial and educational opportunities, planning for the future and avoiding risk may help to achieve this goal. Based in London, Streetwise is a support and counselling service for young people who are involved in any kind of prostitution. It, too, believes that young people need to be given the chance of gaining confidence and self-worth. Its agenda is simple – namely, to put vulnerable people back in touch with their personal power and positive potential: 'We recognise that, through the building of confidence and courage, the self image is healed enough to move towards positive self change' (McMullen, 1987).

Outreach schemes

Much research has demonstrated the difficulties prostitutes experience in using conventional medical services (Barton *et al.*, 1987; Thomson, 1989). They are often reluctant to identify themselves to services such as genito-urinary medicine (GUM) clinics, GPs and social services due to the stigma associated with prostitution and fear of legal recrimination. In Britain, medical outreach schemes for street-working prostitutes have been set up in a number of cities including London, Manchester, Edinburgh, Liverpool and Glasgow. Using a multi-disciplinary approach, they encompass informal drop-in centres, advice lines and mobile services. Outreach methods are valuable for contacting juvenile prostitutes, helping to assess health care needs and referring to appropriate health and social services. Any initial contact can accomplish a great deal of health education work as well as providing young people with supplies of condoms, lubricants and clean injecting equipment. There is also scope for other innovative ways of reaching young people, such as offering contraceptive advice and assertiveness training.

In the Wirral, a multi-disciplinary collaboration between health and youth workers has lead to the successful piloting of a peer education/safer sex project with a group of young female drug users who have also been involved in prostitution. Positive outcomes of the project included the support within the group itself and the enthusiasm of members to share their awareness of the issues discussed with other street workers (Hanslope and Waite, 1994).

In Edinburgh, the Centenary Project runs an outreach clinic for people involved in prostitution. It employs community nurses from varied professional backgrounds (including psychiatry and health visiting) to identify areas of need and to provide and facilitate clinical means of HIV prevention and harm reduction. Promoting health within a group of prostitutes covers a wide area and requires varied knowledge and skills, including education in cervical cytology, contraception, alcohol and drug use, counselling, contact testing and pre- and post-HIV counselling. The team has benefited from training in understanding sexual response and safer sexual practice, in order to improve skills in dealing both with groups of sexually active youngsters and women working in prostitution. The acceptance of the scheme as a safe and confidential environment lead experienced prostitutes to bring new women to the clinic, often young, naive, lonely and scared, for advice in housing and health matters as well as hard facts about the realities of prostitution.

Manchester Action on Street Health (MASH) was formed by a group of professionals and non-statutory workers and funded by the Regional Health Authority. Based in a modern, well-equipped van in the main red-light area, it takes primary health care directly to prostitutes at night, also providing free condoms, needles and syringes as well as a safe place to go for a chat and a cup of coffee. So far, this project has proved a major success and is now expanding into providing emergency contraception, pregnancy testing and genito-urinary services. In addition, it makes referrals to mainstream drug and mental health services, if desired. However, it is important to note that projects such as MASH also serve to perpetuate the alienation of prostitutes from mainstream services by 'reassuring' mainstream health care workers that the problems posed by prostitution are now effectively taken care of. In Manchester, the solution to this dilemma has been to create links between the two sets of workers by releasing volunteers from mainstream services to co-operate with the MASH initiative.

In London, the St Mary's Project for male prostitutes has been set up as a specialist full-time sexual health service for men selling sex to other men. A similar service to that of the Praed Street Project for women, it acts as both a health promotion and education source. The service has strong links with young homeless people and the project offers a drop-in clinic with sessions run by a lawyer and housing agency workers, as well as a 'fast-lane' access to psychologists, trained counsellors and a drug-dependency unit. Its clinical director, David Tomlinson, is currently undertaking research on HIV risk patterns and has already highlighted a dangerous nonchalant attitude from the younger rent boys, which he attributes to economic deprivation, homelessness, despair and a false sense of invulnerability that comes with youth.

In outreach work, it is the clients' needs that set the agenda and health professionals have to use a wide range of knowledge, including previous nursing experience, about general health, midwifery and child care. In addition, the health workers involved must acknowledge that their own values and beliefs may be different from those of their clients, whilst allowing the latter to identify needs and wants according to their own values.

Developing work with drug users

For the drug-using prostitutes in Faugier's (1996) study, the age at which drug use started had a strong influence on their need to prostitute, with 41% of the sample reporting first drug use before the age of 16.

> Simone, aged 17:
> It was me boyfriend who got me into working the streets, like. We were both using drugs and everything, and this was the easy way to make money quick. I didn't know anything about it, and he took me down there, just to see it all, and then I started doing it. It took a while to get used to it; well, at 15, you don't know nothing. It used to make me sick at first; I was real upset. I used to cry all the time; you know, it was like I really felt degraded, and, like, you're using up all your youth. It was a while before I started to blur outside, switch off and not think about it.

The drug-using women represented a younger and much more damaged and vulnerable group than their non drug-using counterparts. They were more likely to have been in care as children and to report sexual abuse, be homeless or living in temporary accommodation which they secured through a sexual relationship. One young woman interviewed was typical of this group: she was 17 years old, pregnant and living in a squat along with six male injecting drug users and a pit bull terrier.

Although the advent of HIV has aroused more interest in drug users, they still remain a very marginalised group of patients in most health care settings. Access to health education and uptake of primary health care have been found to be generally poor or sporadic for drug users (Neville *et al.*, 1988; Milne and Keen, 1988; Datt and Feinmann, 1990). Elion (1990) argues: 'Primary care should be the drug taker's major route to health care, and can be their first and most consistent point of contact with the health care system'. However, the social stigma and illegality attached to illicit drug use and prostitution prevent many young drug-using prostitutes from seeking help with social, health-related and drug problems. Services for the assessment and treatment of young drug misusers are still fragmentary in nature and, where they do exist, appear to lack the will to assume responsibility for tackling this growing problem among the young.

However, this deficiency has been recognised by three agencies in Newcastle-upon-Tyne, where an integrated approach between the Northern Regional Alcohol and Drug Service (NORADS), the Child and Adolescent Psychiatry Service (CAPS) and Streetwise, an independent non-statutory agency, has created a co-operative agency response to the needs of young people. Working together in assessment and treatment processes, with referrals between agencies, has led to the establishment of child protection guidelines and good practice documentation for vulnerable children (Blennerhassett and Gilvarry, 1996).

Street prostitution on a nightly basis to fund a drug habit is likely to bring many of these young people, only a minority of whom are in touch with drug services, into regular contact with the judicial system. The courts can play an important role in identifying children and juveniles at risk due to involvement in drug use and prostitution, and who may be at increased risk of HIV infection and other health care problems. The criminal justice system needs to review the way it addresses the needs of these young people, in order to better identify those concerned, facilitate the implementation of harm reduction strategies and carry out more useful therapeutic interventions with young people during their stay in various institutions (Advisory Council on the Misuse of Drugs, 1991). Providing easy access to health education and medical and drug treatment through community probation services can be an effective way of reaching young people with heavy or chaotic drug-using lifestyles, particularly those with no previous treatment contact (Coleman *et al.*, 1989).

Female prostitutes can also be mothers

Carballo and Rezza (1990) cite repressive policies and condemnatory attitudes as the source of many lost opportunities for health and social services to intervene with drug-using women. Extensive research points to the importance of specialised treatment services in addressing the unique needs of drug-dependent women (Blume, 1990a; 1990b; Marsh and Miller, 1985; Nelson-Zlupko *et al.*, 1995). Henderson (1993) suggests that 'a more user-friendly approach could evolve which moves beyond stereotypes and in so doing "normalises" women who use drugs and commands their effective engagement in reducing harm from their drug use.' Unless services begin to prioritise contact with female drug users, the hidden population will be overburdened with such women, often with children, for whom little help is readily available.

The tendency to withhold knowledge of socially disapproved behaviour from medical and nursing staff is particularly acute among female drug users and stems from a widespread belief that such knowledge is routinely used in child care proceedings. This lack of trust on the part of women combines with the reluctance to treat on the part of primary health care staff and results in a continued abdication of care for women with major health care needs. Female drug users are rarely viewed as the sort of women who should be reproducing and have traditionally faced pressure to terminate pregnancies or to part with children (Ettore, 1992). Stigma and the fear of authorities in turn produce a continued abdication of this specialist care for women (Henderson, 1992). Some specialists in the field of HIV and primary care, such as Bury (1990), suggest that this situation in which female drug users' health care needs remain unmet leads women with HIV infection and AIDS to remain undiagnosed and consequently unable to access appropriate care. These factors continue to pose challenges to health educators and providers of primary health care, as well as specialist drugs and HIV services (Donoghoe *et al.*, 1989; Klee *et al.*, 1990a; 1990b; McKeganey *et al.*, 1993; White *et al.*, 1993). Such attitudes towards women who prostitute and use drugs place their children at risk and only serve to perpetuate the vicious circle of abuse, neglect and deprivation which is often the cause of mothers entering into prostitution and drug abuse in the first place.

Nursing staff, health visitors and midwives form an extremely important professional group in relation to the lives of these women; that is why mainstream services urgently need to carry out adequate assessment of their requirements. Even specialist services, for example, tend to concentrate on the drug abuse problem to the exclusion of all other aspects of clients' lives. One solution lies in the provision of appropriate training on a multi-disciplinary basis in order to link assessment and service delivery. Maternity services are often ill-equipped to work effectively with drug users. Concerned about judgemental reactions and lack of confidentiality, pregnant drug users have been found not to use general health services until late in pregnancy, or not until birth, increasing the health risks for both the mother and child (Klee *et al.*, 1995).

Recently, however, the importance of specialist professional training in this area has been recognised (Department of Health, 1996).

SUMMARY

Juvenile prostitutes have multiple health care needs that are currently poorly addressed by primary health care providers. Situating health care at drug and GUM services may lead to greater uptake generally but many young people do not currently use these services, or they see them as irrelevant to their needs or lifestyles. Primary health care professionals and those working within schools and mainstream services need to develop skills of early recognition and intervention in issues such as substance abuse or suspected prostitution behaviour by children and young people. Health education messages that give top priority to AIDS while ignoring the realities of prostitutes' lives and working conditions stand little chance of being listened to and even less of being acted on. Health care services rarely understand or acknowledge the physical and mental health needs of juvenile prostitutes and until they do, neither the primary nor the secondary specialist services will be able to assist them in combating their drug problems or actively protecting themselves from HIV.

The women interviewed for Faugier's (1996) study expressed feelings of rejection by services which did little to attend to their needs, with primary health care failing almost totally to have any real impact on their health or behaviour. Similarly, secondary services were seen as stigmatising and unhelpful, with few staff understanding the issues or attempting to build rapport. Of most concern was the fact that only very few women had been in contact with specialist drug services and among those who had, the drop-out rate was high, mainly due to the perception that services did not particularly address their needs.

Primary health care workers have an important role to play in encouraging access to specialist services. Multi-disciplinary and cross-boundary working between agencies is vital to ensure a strategic and productive service response to the needs of such young people. Health care professionals cannot operate in isolation or remain on the periphery of vital service provision and understanding of the complex issues affecting these young people. Further outreach work, taking on board the innovative practices of those highlighted in this chapter, is still needed to deliver educational messages to young prostitutes and to enlist their participation in health checks and AIDS prevention strategies.

Intervention strategies should aim to raise the self-esteem of young people, empowering them to make sensible health decisions. Systems also need to be available to adequately prepare young people for when they leave care.

Although it is recognised that innovative ways to encourage HIV risk reduction and improved access to drug treatment and health care are being developed, a greater part could still be played by those involved in primary health care, specialist drug misuse services and the criminal justice system. Within the mainstream services themselves, there is an urgent requirement to carry out adequate assessment of prostitutes' needs. One solution is the provision of appropriate training on a multi-disciplinary basis in order to link assessment and service delivery. Health professionals form an extremely important professional group in relation to the care of these young people.

Role performance and quality of health care depends on the level of education, beliefs and attitudes, and commitment of the health care professionals towards their clients. Currently, lack of expertise and commitment, as well as conflicts between moral stance, personal feelings and legal responsibility, combine to hamper or even prevent positive interventions. Fear and prejudice have a direct effect on the quality of health care and support given to stigmatised individuals. Although the actions of health professionals clearly cannot be divorced from their own social experiences, their personal prejudices need to be recognised and dealt with during the care giving process.

The apparent dearth of current literature available on juvenile prostitutes highlights the importance of more detailed research to explore the realities of their experiences and understand their perceptions of risk. This may facilitate the health care process and help us all understand why children enter into prostitution in the first place.

8. Demystifying Child Prostitution: A Street View

Niki Adams, Claudine Carter, Susan Carter, Nina Lopez-Jones and Cari Mitchell on behalf of the English Collective of Prostitutes

Thousands of children and young people are working as prostitutes to escape rape and other violence in the home and in institutions, and/or to gain some financial independence. This is the result of policies which do not prioritise children's safety and deprive them of income. Once on the game, children, like women, are trapped by laws which make them more vulnerable to violence and brand them as criminals. Abolition of these laws, policies centred on children's needs for economic alternatives and protection from violence, and accountability from professionals, are essential to children's rights, safety and welfare.

MOTHERS AND YOUNG SEX WORKERS TAKE THE LEAD

In 1975, prostitute women occupied churches all over France to protest against police priorities: while the police were doing little about a series of murders and attempted murders of street workers, they had stepped up the arrest of working women. It was the first mass action by prostitute women we know of in recent history. Working women who had participated in, supported, witnessed or been influenced in other ways by the civil rights, national liberation (some of the women were Algerian or had worked in Algeria), students' and factory workers' movements of the 1960s, and the birth of the modern women's movement, were now demanding to be recognised as women and as workers in their own right, and to be protected from violence. Like other mothers, the centrality of children in their lives was clear from their first statement which began, 'These are mothers talking to you ...' and the banner outside the Lyons church, the first to be occupied, which read, 'Our children do not want their mothers in prison' (Jaget, 1980).

Inspired by the French strike, and encouraged by the Wages for

Housework Campaign which had welcomed prostitute women as sisters, two young women, one of them a teenager, started the English Collective of Prostitutes (ECP). As with other young women on the game, they saw prostitution as a way to the financial independence they needed to have some control over their lives. Their insistence that prostitution is a job like any other, better in some ways, worse in others, caused outrage among feminists who accused prostitute women of 'perpetuating sex role stereotypes' and dismay among some older women who were shocked that young women would make this choice.

The ECP's network includes women and girls of different races and backgrounds working at various levels of the sex industry – on the street, in premises, self-employed or employed by others, in strip joints, escort agencies, clubs, on sex lines, etc. – full time, part time or temporary. Although our network is made up mostly of adults, many started to work when they were in their teens or even as young as twelve. Others were not on the game then but were asked for sexual 'favours' by men in their families or who were neighbours. One of the authors of this piece recalls how as a child men bribed her into submitting to their sexual demands:

> I thought granddad was kind to me. My dad, who beat us up, was not kind. Granddad took me out with him, told me stories and sang songs. I soon realised he was kinder to me than to others and that this was to do with our secret games. I thought to let him abuse me was my duty, but also a deal. My rewards were pennies, sweets and walks, often to the pub.

> At age 10 or 11 my friend and I would go to a man's house. He would rub his hands up and down our legs whilst we sat either side of him – and sometimes he'd ask us to walk up and down in front of him 'in a sexy way' and 'show our bums'. For this we'd get money to go swimming or to the pictures or to pay to go on rowing boats at a local pond.

Since the Social Security Act 1986 and the Housing Act 1988, which cut benefits to young people, the number of young women coming to us for help and advice has increased. Denied independent income and housing, young people are either begging, working in prostitution or dependent on others. In our experience, the reasons children and women go into prostitution are similar: to survive; to escape systematic rape or other violence, physical and/or emotional abuse, in the home or in institutions; to have some financial independence and therefore some control over your life. Unlike women, children do not usually have a family to support, although some do contribute to family income or to the support of friends (Stein *et al.*, 1994). Adults often take advantage of children's vulnerability and fear of being sent back. A young man with learning disabilities, who had been raped while in care, told us with obvious pain how he had accepted what seemed to be genuine offers of shelter and companionship by understanding adults, only to find himself working for his adult 'friends' and having to provide them with money as well as free sexual services.

Many children, like many women, go into prostitution to refuse the unlimited emotional and often sexual work that comes with being financially dependent on other people. A sex-for-cash transaction with a minimum of emotional work can be less draining. A young woman had this to say about her relationships before she went on the game:

> Looking back, I realise how much my relationships with men were tied up with the power of money. The way I, and all my friends, behaved to our men was influenced by how we were financially dependent on them. You had to cajole to get a new pair of shoes (while praising him for buying the sexy nightie you never wanted), look nice to be taken out, make him feel good about himself so he didn't spend all the housekeeping on a depressed drunken binge, suffer rape because the house was in his name. The men had pressure on them to provide and took that pressure out on us in varying degrees.

CRIMINALISING PROSTITUTE WOMEN AND CHILDREN

The Children Act 1989 is supposed to have created a framework for the protection of children's rights. But the question still is how to get the police and social services to implement laws which would help protect young people from violence. Professionals are expected to uphold the policies of the government of the day no matter how brutal. This, not the needs of children, determines the priorities of the police and also of the 'caring professions'. In a political climate where children and young people are increasingly portrayed and treated as criminals, adults whose job it is to look after and educate children have been under pressure to police rather than to care. As a grassroots organisation campaigning for the rights of prostitute women, children and men who are among society's most silenced and denigrated workers, we deal with many professionals. Few challenge policies and procedures which keep the power of decision and access to cash and resources out of the hands of those they are supposed to help. Social workers and probation officers who have tried to provide practical help for young people have told us about the opposition they face from managers and even colleagues.

Instead of getting the protection they are entitled to, many children are criminalised by the prostitution laws which take no account of civil rights. The presumption of guilt and the likelihood of false arrest are built into the 1959 Street Offences Act which makes it illegal for a 'common prostitute' – not just any woman – to loiter or solicit for prostitution. A woman or girl is labelled as a 'common prostitute' once she has been given two police cautions, before she ever goes to court. This denies prostitute women and girls the fundamental legal right to be presumed innocent until proven guilty. Unlike others, who are not supposed to be tried on the basis of past convictions, a prostitute woman or girl is judged first of all on her record – not the evidence to prove the charge against her but the previous cautions that label and condemn her. This presumption of guilt is the basis of every conviction for loitering or soliciting.

One would expect that young people under the age of 16 would not be charged with loitering or soliciting. This is not so. Under-16s are routinely cautioned and charged. In some cases, children are told by the police that they will not be charged until they reach the age of 16. According to Home Office figures quoted in *The Game's Up* (Lee and O'Brien, 1995), between 1989 and 1993 there were nearly 1500 convictions and 1800 cautions for prostitution-related offences against young people under 18. The number of cautions issued to girls between 10 and 16 went up by 50% and convictions by 10%. One 10-year-old girl received a caution, four convictions were secured against 12-year-old girls and two against 14-year-old boys. Is it moral for children to face charges under a law framed for adults? And is it legal?

Women and children charged with loitering or soliciting appear in a magistrates' court. The word of a single police officer is the only evidence needed to secure a conviction. Police, courts and often also her solicitor expect her to plead guilty. Magistrates' widespread bias against sex workers ensures that she doesn't get a chance to say much in her own defence and that, even if she does, she is unlikely to be believed. Although fines are supposed to be based on her income, they generally depend on the whim of the magistrate. Young women are regularly fined £100 per charge even when, because they are under 18 and therefore denied benefits, they have no other source of income besides prostitution. The higher the fine, the more punters the young person will have to service in order to pay it.

The 1956 Sexual Offences Act makes it illegal for more than one prostitute woman to advertise and work from the same premises. This promotes red-light areas: by making it almost impossible for prostitute women and clients to contact each other legally, the law forces sex workers into areas known for prostitution where it is easier to make direct contact with clients.

Most teenagers work on the street, which has been estimated by Birmingham-based research to be ten times more dangerous than working from premises (Kinnell, 1993). Unless forced to work for an adult who brings clients to them at his premises, young people do not have the housing or the money to work indoors. Adult sex workers who could provide safer surroundings for girls would thereby risk being done for brothel keeping, procuring for the purposes of prostitution or controlling the movements of a prostitute.

It is also illegal knowingly to permit a person under the age of 18 to enter a sex establishment. Thus, young women aged between 16 and 18 are excluded from the relative safety of working in saunas and massage parlours.

Under the 1956 Act, a man can be charged with living off immoral earnings and a woman with controlling a prostitute if they wholly or partly live off money earned by prostitution. These charges, more than any others, are supposed to protect sex workers from exploitation and violence. But a man cannot be charged with pimping without his victim being labelled a prostitute. This label, in diminishing the victim, diminishes the crime against her.

In our experience, the charge of pimping is more often used against boyfriends or partners in consenting relationships than against real pimps. The police often claim that they cannot arrest pimps because it is difficult to gather evidence against them. 'Police operations against them are expensive and laborious, says the survey ... based on interviews with officers from 29 vice squads. Cases cannot be brought on the uncorroborated word of a prostitute or solely on police evidence' (*Daily Telegraph*, 6 November, 1995).

The anti-rape movement has discredited similar excuses which had been used to justify why so few rapists and violent partners were being arrested. Gathering evidence against pimps is no more difficult than gathering evidence against other violent men – if the will is there. In 1982, we occupied the Church of the Holy Cross in King's Cross for twelve days to protest against the police acting illegally by arresting women when they were not working and singling out black sex workers (James, 1983; English Collective of Prostitutes, 1997). A number of working women complained to councillors who visited the church that the police had not moved against pimps who had threatened the women with violence. It appeared to some of the women that the police targeted for arrest those who worked independently of pimps. Other people have noted a closer relationship between police and pimps than between police and prostitutes:

> Last year, a BBC North programme on under-age prostitution in
> Middlesbrough showed that the treatment of pimps by the police
> seemed to be very lax and even bordered on friendly; and that men in
> the cars were simply cautioned. Meanwhile, the girls were finger-
> printed, cautioned and criminalised by being known as a 'common
> prostitute. (*THE GUARDIAN*, 22 August, 1996)

Introduced in the 1985 Sexual Offences Act, kerb crawling legislation criminalised street clients for the first time. Although it was said to be aimed at men, women and girls were its first victims. It has made sex workers, especially those who are young and less experienced, more vulnerable to violence as they have less time to check out a client who is worried about being arrested before jumping into his car.

PROSTITUTION: ONE WAY TO REFUSE RAPE

In campaigning against criminalisation, we have refused to disconnect the situation of children working as prostitutes from that of women, which would have mystified the children's situation. There are, of course, important differences between them, stemming from the fact that children have even less economic and social power and even fewer rights than women, both as victims of violence and as illegal workers.

Children who report rape or sexual assault (and the great majority are not in a position to say anything) are still even less likely to be believed and protected than women who have been raped. The rape of children is not called that: it is usually referred to as incest or sexual abuse, a clear indication that, despite righteous public statements, the authorities and the media do not treat it seriously – they do not intend to 'throw money at it' and thoroughly monitor adults in authority (Women Against Rape, forthcoming).

Prostitution is sex work, whatever the differences when adults or children do it. It may not be a great job, especially for children who should not have to work for survival and who are less protected by the state and society generally, and less experienced in protecting themselves. But prostitution can be the best of a set of bad choices. People are horrified that children are selling sex for £15 or less but young people are among the lowest paid workers, with few employment rights, long hours and exhausting jobs. Often the only work available is 'cash-in-hand' with no legal protection. Prostitution can seem much less work for better pay than any other work available.

Research confirms that the financial exploitation of children has increased in the past few years:

> Under-18s are the only group in Britain whose average weekly wage has fallen since 1992. Wages before tax for young men fell by nearly 1 per cent to £112.80 and for women there was a drop of 5.9 per cent to £103.30. The Youth Training Allowance has been frozen at £29.50 a week for 16-year-olds since 1989 and £35 for 17-year-olds since 1986. In 1988, all welfare payments to 16- and 17-year-olds were axed.
> (*OBSERVER*, 23 July, 1995)

The choices open to children are often to do housework and child care for women, or housework and sex work for men:

> Sometimes I stayed with women who had young children. I'd look after the kids and keep house in exchange for a place to stay and food and sometimes a bit of cash to go to the local teenage discos. When I found an older boyfriend I stayed with him in his bedsit, washed his clothes and had sex regularly. I felt very grown up and free, though looking back it doesn't seem so liberating!

> Others find jobs where there is accommodation, such as au pairing, nannying, nursing, working in holiday camps or pub work. In many of these jobs, young women are expected to provide a sexual service for the employers or the customers, but this sex work is not part of the job description. You are expected to provide a sexual service in a context where someone else controls your life. Sometimes your entire life is

taken up with the work. In prostitution the pay is better and once the sex is done you can be detached and independent, your life can be more your own.

TRAPPED BY A CRIMINAL RECORD

The National Association of Young People in Care has exposed and publicised the extent of rape and other institutional violence against young people (Moss *et al.*, 1990). This organising and other resistance by young people has changed the climate of silence which imprisoned children in 'respectable' families like that of the Wests or in 'caring' institutions described by the Chair of Clwyd Social Services, Malcolm King, as 'a Gulag archipelago stretching across Britain' (*Independent on Sunday*, 10 March, 1996). The media now loves 'child abuse scandals'. But little has changed for children. The concerns expressed about children in sex work are often hollow. They rarely extend to real help and are themselves a smoke screen for the absence of alternatives. What help is there for children who want to leave prostitution but do not want to be sent back to their families or into care?

A criminal record and the stigma attached to the job institutionalise women and children in prostitution: it is much harder to leave if you are denied entry to another job or a college course because you have a record for prostitution or because you have to hide the job experience you have and therefore appear not to have any experience. Even though prostitution involves consenting sex, the Home Office records offences of loitering, soliciting or brothel keeping as sexual offences – like rape. On this basis, women who have a record for prostitution, which often they got as teenagers, have been refused access to social work courses or jobs, especially if these involve working with children. Far from protecting children, the prostitution laws ensure criminalisation at an earlier age.

Unfortunately, in our experience child welfare organisations are not always ready to tackle child poverty and criminalisation, and because of this their proposals can in our view be damaging. For example, the report *Splintered Lives* (Kelly *et al.*, 1995) launched in February 1996 by five children's charities, shies away from supporting The Children's Society's campaign for the decriminalisation of child prostitution and the reinstatement of benefits for under 18s. Instead, it endorses the tightening of immigration controls against unaccompanied children and calls for 'special courts and prosecutors'. Such measures reinforce police powers rather than children's right to protection and promote legislation against sex tour operators which relies on charges of 'conspiracy' rather than actual violence, and is therefore open to abuse. Special courts would downgrade violence against women and children just like the prostitution laws have downgraded violence against those of us working as prostitutes – separate is never equal.

WORKING TOGETHER

The media often claim that older women are hostile to younger women coming into the industry. They also claim that 'local' women are against 'outsiders' – sometimes black women who are local are also considered 'outsiders'. As with all groups, antagonisms exist; in our experience, those among prostitutes are often fuelled by the police. Before our church occupation, the police tried to set white women against black women, asking the white women to grass on the black women in exchange for not getting arrested. At other times the police tell women that kids ready to turn a trick for a meal or a fix are the 'real problem'.

In fact, women often take care of each other, working out a security system among themselves. Older women are concerned that children and younger women on the game may bring the prices down by increasing competition. But they are also concerned that children and younger women may be particularly vulnerable to violence, arrest and exploitation. Some young women have been sent to us by older women alarmed by how little help and support they were getting.

In July 1996, Kay Mellor, creator of the television series *Band of Gold*, and Geraldine James, who plays the older prostitute, Rose, appeared at a benefit for us where they discussed their series with the audience. One of the most talked about characters was that of 16-year-old Tracy, who kills herself after confronting her father who had sexually abused her from the age of eleven. To escape this violence, Tracy runs away from home and ends up on the game. Although her life in prostitution is hard and violent, she also builds caring and supportive relationships with some of the other women, especially with Rose, who takes her under her wing, and Collette, a young lesbian. Unlike her mother and sister, who doubt her when she tells them about the abuse she has suffered at her father's hands, her sex worker friends believe her. Such solidarity is common among women and children at the bottom whose experience of being raped or assaulted, and then disbelieved and ignored by people in authority, is collectively taken for granted and much more likely to be openly discussed.

PROTECTING CHILDREN AND CHILDREN'S RIGHTS

Unlike organisations which are funded to 'rehabilitate' young people out of prostitution, we take it as our job to demystify government policies which result in child prostitution. Lack of care, as well as rape and other violence in children's homes, homelessness, denial of benefits and protection, and the persecution and criminalisation of young people when they come out of care, force children into prostitution and institutionalise them there.

We are frequently contacted for advice and help by young people, their families or friends, social workers and other professionals. Doing the work of finding out what young people need and want, and getting people in positions of authority to provide such entitlements, has shaped our campaigning. We have been pressing for resources such as housing, benefits and police protection to give young people the choice to leave prostitution. This can mean persuading social workers or probation officers to use their power to keep the young person out of the criminal justice system.

Police enforcement of the prostitution laws is often illegal – we have defended women and children from malicious arrests, false charges, persecution, threats and intimidation by police officers. The 'special attention' children get usually amounts to special harassment: children are arrested over and over again in an attempt to force them off the streets at any cost, even locking them up in secure units. In our experience, not many social workers are ready to challenge or even acknowledge that the police break the law. For example, in October 1993 we were contacted by a 16-year-old girl from the home counties. Ms Z was working on the street and the police were arresting and cautioning her all the time. Shortly after, we got a call from an older woman working the same beat who was horrified at how the police were treating Ms Z. She had been arrested nine times in one month and the police had told her that they were arresting her in preference to other women and that as soon as she was 17 they were going to charge her. They were insulting and abusive, calling her a slag and other names. On one occasion when in custody, they claimed she was suicidal and threatened to lock her up 'elsewhere' rather than in a detention cell. Many of her friends were prostitutes and she was often arrested when she was with them, even when she wasn't working. Her boyfriend, even when they were out for the evening, was often stopped and questioned by the vice squad. After four months of unrelenting harassment, the police told her that they would stop arresting her if she agreed to become a police informant.

Ms Z's situation is common. Her Income Support had been cut off. The police did not do anything to help her get it reinstated; we did. We also helped her get housing benefit so that she could move into a new flat, leave the area and leave prostitution if she chose.

In May 1996, a family care worker called us about a 14-year-old girl who had been working for over a year. She said that she had gone into prostitution because her parents, who were on disability benefits and a pension, could not afford to give her any money and she 'wanted some independence'. She had made a 'contract' with her family to be home by 11 p.m. at night. At the case conferences organised to discuss her situation, the 'deterrent' proposed by the police was to target her: arrest her every time she came out onto the street. Their other proposal was to lock her up in a secure unit. There was no justification for locking the girl up in a secure unit – she was not a danger to herself or to others and was happy living with her family. We discussed with the family care worker how she could prevent this happening. What would have happened if the social worker had not consulted us and not been respectful of the girl's needs and wishes?

In our experience, the main police concern is that children and young people should not be visibly on the streets; young people's situations, the violence they may be escaping from or may face if they are forced out of view, seem not to be given much weight. Such indifference cannot be based on ignorance – many officers know exactly what children are running away from. From our Women's Centre in the red-light area of King's Cross, London, we witnessed and opposed for years countless police crackdowns: under the guise of 'cleaning up' the streets of prostitution and drug dealing, homeless people, beggars and prostitutes, many in their teens are arrested, evicted and moved out of the area.

How the police treat young prostitute women and men is not so unlike their treatment of young people in general: widespread stop and search, particularly of black teenagers, and the dismissal of racist attacks. One woman recalls:

> When I was 13, I was beaten up by racists in the street. I went to the police, they left me waiting in the corridor out the back. A sergeant shouted at me for sitting on the floor, 'You, girl, what the hell do you think you're doing? Get up. Show some respect.' I knew I wasn't going to get any help there, that he didn't see me as anything of importance, I was young and black. I left.

Cases such as the West murders or the Dunblane massacre generate great media debates about the 'evil' of human nature. But what about the 'evil' of authorities which repeatedly ignore complaints, reports and other signs of violence against children? Neither West nor Hamilton was unknown to the police.

In 1995, we became involved with the mothers of two murdered teenagers after we protested about an article which absolved the police of any responsibility for preventing the murders. This is what one of the mothers told us.

At 15, Ms Y started a relationship with a man who was violent to her. Her mother went to social services for help. Two social workers visited and told her mother there was nothing they could do because she was 'like any other young woman that age'. The mother asked, 'Are you waiting for her to become a prostitute, get hooked on drugs and get murdered before you are ready to do something?' At 16, Ms Y left home to live with her boyfriend. He continued to beat her up and forced her to work as a prostitute. When her mother intervened he threatened her. Ms Y called the police on a number of occasions. They told her they could only do something if she was ready to make a statement and take him to court but as is usual they offered her no protection.

In May 1994, Ms Y was murdered – one of at least seven young women murdered in the Midlands during that period, most of them in their late teens or early twenties. Her mother describes trying to find out what had happened to her daughter: 'I did all the 'phoning, the police told me nothing.' Her daughter's body was returned to her in a plastic bag marked 'health hazard, do not view' because the body had begun to rot. Ms Y's murderer has not been found and her mother's enquiries to the police are met with, 'We are doing all we can'.

The police do have the power to help and prevent crime, even murder. Some years ago, we met a working woman who was terrified because her ex-partner, who was in prison for a series of violent attacks against her and had sworn to kill her, was due out. The woman could not hide because her child, who had a disability, could not be moved from a special school. She had resigned herself to the fact that her murder was inevitable. Refusing to accept that nothing could be done, we asked to meet with her and her probation officer. We suggested that the probation officer should contact the local MP before contacting the police. As a result of this pressure, the police installed a panic button at the woman's house, which they had never offered before, and agreed to be in constant touch with her.

The man came after her as soon as he was out but she immediately alerted the police – he was arrested and sent back to prison. This convinced her that she was not doomed and showed her ex-partner that he'd better stay away.

There are many practical measures which would help women and children to escape from violent partners, fathers, stepfathers, etc. Priorities and resources are always the issue. We have got women and their children rehoused in different areas or towns where their attackers would not find them, but this would not have happened if we hadn't pressed the police, social workers, councillors and MPs, and sometimes also contacted the press.

Children complaining about rape or other violence are less likely to be believed than adults. If they are runaways they won't be able to go to the police because they would be returned to the family or institution where they suffered the violence in the first place. They have to continue to work on the street, avoiding the police but within easy reach of violent men.

Although the pimping laws are supposed to protect women and children from violence and exploitation, they encourage both. They do not distinguish between partners women have chosen to be with and pimps who impose themselves. In this way, the laws mystify sex workers' family relationships as intrinsically violent: people can't see that the violence prostitute women face from their partners is no different from, no better or worse than, the domestic violence many other women face. Like prostitutes, other women and children are also trapped in violent situations, raped and robbed of their money by violent partners or relatives who drink or gamble it away. The difference is that prostitute women and children are criminalised, stigmatised and isolated by the very laws which claim to protect them, and are therefore more vulnerable to pimping.

Teenagers try very hard to work independently of pimps. If they succeed, it is because of great resourcefulness. They stay away from the police as much as they can, fearful of investigations which may do more harm than good. Investigations can quickly become an occasion for the police to collect information about particular individuals and communities for purposes other than the violence at hand. This discourages anyone who may want to give information from coming forward for fear of involvement in other matters or even being accused of something else.

For example, a woman who ran away as a teenager told us how racism prevents victims like herself from coming forward:

The stereotype of the helpless white victim and the violent black pimp often held me back from reporting violence as I felt I couldn't trust the police not to be racist. Black men are not more violent than white men nor more likely to be pimps, but they are more likely to be stereotyped. So are black prostitute women:

> I experienced violence for ten years. When my pimp's other 'girlfriend' and I got together to report him and offered to testify in court, the police were not interested. They said they were getting him for 'something more important'. We were not called to give evidence and he only got eight months.

Street sweeps make it more dangerous for women and children to work, driving them further underground or into unfamiliar neighbourhoods where they have no support network – one of the women murdered in the Midlands had recently been driven out of Wolverhampton to Stoke-on-Trent where she was killed.

Around the time of Ms Y's murder, we wrote to MPs and councillors asking them to support our call for police action which targeted the Midlands murderer/s, and for protection and a temporary amnesty to potential victims and witnesses. The police responded with more street sweeps: apparently the lives of prostitute women and children didn't count for much. This encourages men who hate women and/or children, and vigilantes anxious to increase the value of their property by ridding the area of people who work or live on the streets – homeless people, beggars, sex workers.

In Balsall Heath, Birmingham, vigilantes have been patrolling the streets for over two years. Sex workers reported to us, and in the press, that they were physically attacked by the vigilantes: 'I was dragged into a car by a gang of men and called a slag and a slut. I have never been so scared' (*Birmingham Post*, 20 July, 1994). Other residents have also protested against 'the rule of vigilantes': 'As a young woman, I have never felt threatened by prostitutes in my street. The same is not true of the "pickers" who gather on the street corners: obscenities have been shouted in my direction; lewd suggestions addressed to me; placards waved, including "Your [sic] dead prostitute" ... recently, on my way home, I was threatened with a knife by the "pickers" ' (*Observer*, 24 July, 1994). Although the police say they take all complaints seriously, vigilante violence has been legitimised as 'community action' and the vigilantes have been issued with police registration cards.

The police are not the only ones to dismiss violence against sex workers. Often the Crown Prosecution Service (CPS) will not prosecute. In May 1995, two prostitute women set a legal precedent: with our help and the help of Legal Action for Women (LAW) and Women Against Rape (WAR), the women brought the first private prosecution for rape in England and Wales after the CPS dropped their case. The man was sentenced to 14 years (reduced to 11 years on appeal) on the same evidence the CPS had dismissed as insufficient. One of the women told the court that when she first reported the rape, two policewomen discouraged her from making a statement: they told her she didn't have much chance of having the man prosecuted because it was a prostitute's word against his. The private prosecution is a turning point in the movements against rape and for sex workers' rights. It sets a precedent for everyone struggling to get justice.

Just before the private prosecution came to trial, LAW and WAR jointly published *Dossier: The Crown Prosecution Service and the Crime of Rape* (1995) which documents 14 other rape cases where, despite good evidence, the CPS refused to prosecute. Five of the 14 victims (over one third) were children at the time of the attack. The children were all raped in the home. The CPS has denied any bias in its decisions not to prosecute. But the facts in these 14 cases tell a different story. In all the cases, the victims had a lower social status than their attackers on the basis of sex, age, race or disability. This explains in part why only one in 200 rapists is successfully prosecuted (Hall, 1985; LAW and WAR, 1995).

COMPENSATION

The Criminal Injuries Compensation Board (CICB) has discretionary powers to discriminate against victims who work as prostitutes and their families, denying or lowering compensation on grounds of 'character or conduct'. Prostitute women and children (including those who have no convictions) and their families, are among the first to be denied compensation.

Ms Y's mother applied to the CICB for compensation for her daughter's murder and for financial help with the costs of raising Ms Y's son who was a year old when he lost his mother. She was told that she would have been eligible for £3000 and the child for £7000 but that because Ms Y was working as a prostitute at the time of her murder, neither of them would get anything. In addition to losing his mother, the child has to deal with the authorities whose decision condemns not the violence but the victim.

The CICB's refusal to compensate Ms Y's mother and son for her murder is typical of their widespread bias against sex workers and their families. Another woman who was violently assaulted, raped and robbed as a teenager was refused compensation because she had convictions related to prostitution. She won £4000 after we helped prepare her case and Women Against Rape represented her at the appeal hearing. (English Collective of Prostitutes, 1996; Women Against Rape, 1996).

Forty young people who were raped or sexually abused in children's homes were refused compensation because of offences committed after, and as a result of, the violence they had suffered. They had to appeal to get the decision quashed. Even then, the amounts awarded for buggery on numerous occasions over a period of two or three years are small.

WHAT CAN BE DONE

Our demands have remained basically the same since 1975:

- abolition of the prostitution laws which criminalise sex workers, including children;

- recognition of sex workers as workers with legal, economic and civil rights, including the right to police protection from rape and other violence;

- safe houses to which young people can escape from their torturers and receive the protection and care they are entitled to;

- no ghettoes such as legalised brothels or toleration zones – separate is never equal;

- economic alternatives to prostitution – higher benefits, grants and wages, and housing and other resources – so that no woman, child or man is forced by poverty into sex with anyone. Then and now, we are 'For Prostitutes, Against Prostitution'.

We now add:

- the reinstatement of benefits to young people – they provide a vital alternative to prostitution and the beginning of economic independence;

- the reinstatement of education grants – some of the young people in our network support their studies by working in prostitution;

- the end of loitering, soliciting and brothel-keeping offences being recorded as sexual offences along with rape, since this bars young people and women who have such records from jobs, particularly those involving children;

- the abolition of Paragraph 6(c) on Character and Conduct from the Criminal Injuries Compensation Board guidelines which institution-alises prejudice into compensation decisions. Compensation should be based on evidence about the attack and its effects, not on prejudices or moralising about the victim's occupation, 'way of life', sex, race, class, disability, immigration or other legal status, age, sexual prefer-ence, etc.

Prostitute women and children trapped in violent situations need what any one of us who is facing violence needs: resources to escape, and police, social services and courts prioritising our safety. There is increasing support for this view, from groups as diverse as The Chil-dren's Society to the Task Force on Prostitution set up by the City of San Francisco, whose final report launched in August 1996 recommends decriminalisation, shelters and independent housing, and a whole range of services for young people in prostitution (The San Francisco Task Force on Prostitution, 1996).

9. Causes of Youth Prostitution, New Forms of Practice and Political Responses

John Pitts

In this chapter I shall explore the connections between poverty, sexual abuse and the involvement of children and young people in prostitution. Clearly, not every child or young person who is impoverished or sexually abused will become involved in prostitution. On the other hand, there is evidence that poverty and sexual abuse together correlate very closely with such involvement. I shall argue that youth prostitution is both a survival strategy and a way of exerting some control, albeit in a transitory and potentially dangerous form, for young people who often believe that their lives are beyond their control (Seng, 1989). Seen from this perspective, it is possible to conceive of interventions which offer alternative modes of survival and different sources of control. But it also suggests new forms of professional practice and political organisation, at a local level, which could counter the pressures towards involvement in prostitution and offer alternatives to potentially destructive familial relationships and social roles.

LORD WOLFENDEN AND THE DISAPPEARING PROSTITUTE

Despite the profound social changes which have occurred in this country during the past 40 years, official responses to prostitution are still influenced by the values and assumptions which shaped the Wolfenden Committee's report on Homosexual Offences and Prostitution published in 1957. Rather than attempting to prohibit homosexuality and prostitution, Wolfenden aimed to render them invisible by putting them behind closed doors. For Wolfenden these were private matters, contracts which, when freely entered by consenting adults, were no business of the state. The report aimed to draw a clearer distinction between the law and morality, eradicate the affront to public decency which these activities were deemed to represent and in doing so, rationalise the control of street prostitution (Matthews, 1986). Whereas the origins of drug use, youth crime and child abuse have been the subject of considerable official attention in the intervening period, official responses to child and youth prostitution are still characterised by Wolfenden's suppression of the visible and tolerance of the invisible.

RECESSION AND THE RESURGENCE OF STREET PROSTITUTION

For some time Wolfenden's reforms were extremely successful in clearing the streets of prostitution (Swingler, 1969; Cunnington, 1980). However, as the economic recession which began at the end of the 1960s deepened, many women, particularly those in unskilled, seasonal and non-unionised occupations were expelled from the labour market and placed in a situation of enforced dependency upon dwindling welfare benefits. This 'feminisation' of poverty was exacerbated by heightened levels of family breakdown and a consequent increase in the number of single-parent families. As Matthews (1986) has observed:

> Under these conditions it is not surprising that prostitution becomes an increasingly attractive option – or rather a decreasingly unattractive option – for many women resulting, as a number of observers noted, in the growing incidence of street walking. Thus the removal of the visible and public spectre of women on the streets, which many had considered Wolfenden's central achievement, was gradually being overturned as more and more women took to the streets. Not only were street walkers becoming more numerous, but they also appeared to be getting younger.

Like their older counterparts, this new wave of children and young people taking to the streets was also a victim of social change and economic recession. However, the plight of these young people was compounded in the 1980s and 1990s by neo-conservative economic policies which reduced the capacity of families to support their children, and neo-conservative social policies which reduced the capacity of the social security system, voluntary and statutory social service agencies, and the education and youth services, to respond to those children when they found themselves in difficulties (Currie, 1991).

CHILDREN ON THE STREET

In 1975, the television documentary *Johnny Go Home* caused a public outcry when it revealed that every night in London, 2000 runaway children could be found on the streets. More worryingly, it showed that some of these children were victims of highly organised paedophile rings. The programme triggered action in the voluntary sector to respond to the plight of these young people and some government funding was redirected towards this work. *Johnny Go Home* also gave impetus to attempts within the voluntary sector and the police to discover the nature and size of the problem of young runaways. A Children's Society estimate, based on a survey of minors reported missing in 53 UK police districts between 1983 and 1986 (Newman, 1989) put the figure at 98,000 per annum. A later study, undertaken by National Children's Homes (Abrahams and Mungall, 1992), analysed the cases of 17,000 young people reported missing in five areas. The study indicated that although an estimated 43,000 children leave home each year 'to escape warring parents, beatings, sexual abuse, poverty and boredom', most ran only a few miles and two-thirds returned home of their own volition, four out of five within 48 hours. The study revealed that most runaways were aged between 14 and 16, although an estimated 3000 were aged only 11.

NEIGHBOURHOOD DECLINE, POVERTY, FAMILY STRESS AND RUNNING AWAY

Hope (1994) observes that between 1981 and 1991 poverty and social deprivation in the UK were progressively redistributed towards what had become, in effect, urban ghettos characterised by burgeoning problems of crime, violence and drug abuse. This 'South-Africanisation' of the city (Davis, 1990) was a product of the housing and social security policies of the 1980s and the radical redistribution of wealth in favour of the prosperous which characterised that decade. These developments were, of course, paralleled by a growth in youth unemployment, youth crime, youth homelessness, youth suicide and youth prostitution (Stein *et al.*, 1994). These neighbourhoods were often the most rundown council estates and, during the 1980s, the average income of council households fell from 75% of the national average to 49% (Hope, 1994). A study commissioned by the Joseph Rowntree Foundation (1996) found that by 1995, 50% of council dwellings had no wage earner. These neighbourhoods were 'destabilised' by rapid population shifts in which older, relatively prosperous residents, often in skilled employment, moved out to be replaced by young, low-income families. The relative unemployability of this new population led to the erosion of its links with the local economy and this served to compound the social isolation of residents. Their plight was exacerbated by the flight of businesses and industries to new sites on the periphery of cities and the progressive erosion and transformation of public services (Pitts, 1995).

These are the areas where, from the early 1980s, young men who in a previous era would have grown out of crime, simply didn't (McGahey, 1986). These are also the neighbourhoods which witnessed a steady increase in racist attacks, periodic small-scale riots and drug-related crime and violence. Pearson (1987) notes that:

> By the mid-1980s, the official number of heroin addicts had increased alarmingly by British standards to more than twelve thousand. It is a fair guess that the actual number of heroin users in Britain by this time was well in excess of 50,000 and possibly between 60,000 and 80,000.

Importantly, Pearson found that opiate abuse tended to infuse whole neighbourhoods as a collective solution to a shared problem:

> Even within a town or city with a major problem it will tend to be concentrated in certain neighbourhoods and virtually unknown in others. Moreover where the problem has tended to gather together in dense pockets within our towns and cities, this will usually be in neighbourhoods which are worst affected by unemployment and wretched housing.

Not surprisingly perhaps, they are also the areas from which young people are most likely to run away. In his study of 1158 first admissions to a London safe house for young runaways, Pitts (1992) noted that whereas 458 of these children came from London and the South East, 356 came from regions characterised by economic stagnation, high unemployment and family poverty. A recent survey undertaken by the youth homelessness charity Centrepoint (1995) echoes these findings (cf. Table 1 below).

Table 1: County of origin of homeless young people from outside London using Centrepoint projects* between April 1994 and March 1995

Home Counties		Other Regions	
Surrey	3	Durham	6
Bucks	3	Cheshire	7
Berks	3	South Yorkshire	7
Sussex	4	Northern Ireland	8
Kent	4	Strathclyde	10
Hants	9	Merseyside	11
Herts	4	Greater Manchester	15
Essex	6	West Midlands	15
Total	**36**		**79**

*Berwick Street, Buffey House, Breakspear Road, Delancy, Haberdasher's House, Intake, Housing Team, Vauxhall. (Off The Street did not provide data for the whole year so total figures may be an underestimate.)

Source: Centrepoint Statistics 1995

The discrepancy between relatively prosperous and relatively impoverished areas also emerges from an analysis of young people from the London boroughs who constituted 56% of admissions to the Centrepoint projects between April 1994 and March 1995 (cf. Table 2 below). Only 65 came from the relatively prosperous outer London boroughs, while 436 came from inner London, with most coming from those boroughs with the highest levels of social deprivation and youth and adult unemployment.

In his study of young people running from home in Luton in 1992, Shriane (1995) found that 42% ran from one housing estate located in the electoral ward scoring highest on indices of social deprivation and social problems (Wells and Berridge, 1995). This estate was the scene of serious rioting in 1995. Graham and Bowling (1995), in their study of young people and crime, found a strong correlation between family poverty, strained family relationships and the family's capacity to supervise its children. Of the young people entering the Centrepoint projects in 1994/95, 18% had been told to leave the parental home or were evicted, 25% had left as a result of family arguments, 13% had left as a result of 'relationship breakdown', while 8% cited physical violence and 2% sexual violence. Currie (1991) has argued that economic recession and low levels of benefit have placed enormous strains upon poor families. Not only are poor parents who spend time with their children penalised by the benefits system, that system also keeps some women, and therefore their children, locked into a state of economic dependency upon abusive men. Poor relationships with step-parents accounted for a significant proportion of the family conflict reported in Graham and Bowling's study and this correlated closely with running away, although problems of conflict between children and their step-parents are not simply a product of low family income, of course.

Table 2: Borough of origin of homeless London young people using Centrepoint projects* (see note in Table 1) between April 1994 and March 1995

Outer London Boroughs		Inner London Boroughs	
Havering	1	City	1
Kingston	1	Kensington & Chelsea	12
Sutton	1	Greenwich	13
Bexley	2	Tower Hamlets	14
Enfield	2	Waltham Forest	14
Hillingdon	2	Haringey	15
Merton	2	Newham	16
Harrow	3	Camden	21
Bromley	4	Wandsworth	21
Hounslow	4	Westminster	24
Barking	5	Hammersmith	28
Redbridge	6	Brent	33
Barnet	9	Hackney	33
Ealing	11	Islington	35
Croydon	12	Southwark	40
		Lewisham	40
		Lambeth	76
Total	65		436

Source: Centrepoint Statistics 1995

RUNNING OUT OF CARE

The NCH study cited above (1992) established that one-third of runaway children ran from local authority care. This is a remarkable figure when we recognise that children in local authority care constitute no more than 1% of the age group. The NCH findings echo those of Pitts (1992) who found that 36% of first admissions to a London safe house ran from care and that children in care ran more frequently. He writes:

> A significant difference between the Care and the non-Care populations was the number of times they had run away. Less than 10% of the youngsters from Care had never run away before, against 37% of the non-Care population. The proportion of people in Care who had run away more than five times, 48%, was well in excess of the non-Care population, 18%.

He also notes that the older the child, the more likely they were to have run from care, with three-quarters of 17-year-old self-referrals to the safe house having run from care. This is not surprising since, as Bullock and Millham (1989) found, the majority of children and young people in care are adolescents; 70% are over the age of ten and a quarter are over 16. Of the young people entering the Centrepoint projects in 1994/95, 28% had previously been the subject of care orders.

From the early 1970s, as a result of changing professional orthodoxies and dwindling financial resources, the residential child care system in the UK began to shrink. This shrinkage accelerated rapidly in the 1980s as wave after wave of government cutbacks took their toll. In this period, the last residential nurseries, virtually all of the community homes (with education), the erstwhile approved schools and most local authority children's homes were closed down. This left a residual 'system' of residential care, provided in large part by small private and voluntary organisations.

This paucity of residential provision has meant that placements have tended to be made on the basis of desperation rather than deliberation (Segal and Schwartz, 1987). In the late 1980s, one inner London local authority was eventually forced to place a 15-year-old young woman, who had been taken into care because she was thought to be involved in prostitution, in a bedsit in the heart of the red-light area beside King's Cross station. This desperation appears to characterise both initial placements and placements for children returned to local authority care after running away. A one-month follow-up study undertaken at the London safe house between June 1985 and June 1987 revealed that 70% of the children were returned to the place from which they had run (Pitts, 1992).

Whereas 43% of the children placed back at home ran away again within the month, 62% of the care population did so, and as Pitts (1992) observes, 'This suggested that these people were being returned to unsatisfactory and possibly high risk situations'.

FOSTERING A GRUDGE

The decline of residential provision was paralleled by an expansion of the child and adolescent fostering schemes operated by local authorities. The many positive aspects of these developments notwithstanding, they have often meant that little, if any, choice is available to adolescents entering the care of the local authority. In a county in the south east of England which had closed most of its residential units, young people who persistently 'broke down' in foster placements were eventually referred to the county's adolescent psychiatric unit because it was the only available residential facility. In Warwickshire, the wholesale closure of children's homes in 1986 left the authority with no residential services of its own. In his study of these developments, Cliffe (1990) noted that:

> Most children were offered only one choice of foster placement and, obviously, no residential placement – in other words, no choice at all. Secondly, although Warwickshire has shown that more difficult children can be fostered than was previously thought, there is still a small group – mostly adolescent boys – who need residential placements.

Crimmens (1991), who was project leader of a London safe house in the late 1980s, has observed that:

> One major problem presented by young runaways from Care is the breakdown of foster placements. These young people often state quite clearly that they do not want to live in a family. They have families of their own which they may, or may not, return to. They do not want the pressures of family life, other adults 'pretending to be your mum and dad', or simply to live in a situation in which they feel they have failed. What they want is a 'good children's home'.

LEAVING CARE

Of the young people entering the Centrepoint projects in 1994/95, 28% had previously been the subject of a care order and 51% of those who had been in residential care had run away from it before they were 16. In a study of 39 care leavers, Centrepoint established that 56% of them had been homeless immediately after leaving care, that nearly all of them had slept rough and that 30% had become homeless when social work support was withdrawn (Kirby, 1995). The experience of residential care is often disabling for adolescents because it results in 'further separations, attenuation of family ties and discontinuity' (Kufeldt, 1991). The findings of Berridge and Cleaver (1987) alert us to the fact that health and educational needs, as well as family contact, become secondary to the stabilisation of the placement. Not surprisingly then, children leaving care are not only more prone to (often undiagnosed or neglected) problems of mental and physical health (Kirby, 1995; Stiffman *et al.*, 1988), they also have far fewer sources of emotional and material support and far fewer skills and educational qualifications with which to make their way in the world than other young people. The majority of those interviewed in the Centrepoint study felt that they had been given little or no preparation for leaving care and few had been given advice or training on specific independent living skills. This had the effect of putting onto the street ill-prepared, poorly educated and emotionally fragile young people, many of whom had been received into care in the first place because of abuse, neglect, self-harm, or their violent or aggressive behaviour (Kirby, 1995).

STREET LIFE

Centrepoint estimates that within six weeks, most young people living on the street will resort to crime, drugs and/or prostitution as a survival strategy (Kirby, 1995). In their study, Yates *et al.* (1988) found that 84% of runaway youths used drugs and alcohol, and that 34.5% of this group had taken drugs intravenously. Pitts (1992) found that 16% of the children and young people admitted to a London safe house had used illegal drugs. The initial vulnerability of these young people has been compounded in the 1980s by the government's social security reforms. In April 1988, state benefits were withdrawn from young people under 18 living away from the parental home. This confronted many of them with a stark choice between returning to the parental home or moving onto the streets. A survey conducted by Centrepoint in the eight months following the implementation of the 1988 Social Security Act indicated that the numbers of 16- to 19-year-olds without proper accommodation in London had increased by 35% over the period. Their plight was worsened by major changes to the board and lodgings regulations in 1989 and changes in the funding arrangements for housing association hostels in the 1989 Housing Act. These problems were compounded by the introduction of the poll tax, which provided a massive disincentive to private landlords. Of the young people entering the Centrepoint projects in 1994/95, 41% had no source of income and 43% were receiving no state benefits. Beyond this, as West (1988) notes:

> Private housing is rationed by the openly discriminatory practices of many landlords, together with the physical condition and demand for money up-front. Open discrimination includes refusal to take as tenants certain individuals – for example those who are unemployed, black, male, female, gay, under 20 and so on. In addition, the number of young women offered flats in return for sex or sex in lieu of rent is increasing.

Homeless young people also confront the 1996 Housing Act which threatens the eligibility of vulnerable homeless people for permanent housing. It will also end the priority lists of homeless people in need and the special allowances for which people with priority needs are currently eligible. Amanda Allard, Policy Officer at The Children's Society, has observed that 'without a legal requirement, housing departments are unlikely to nominate voluntarily the tenancies needed for Care leavers.' (Easton, 1996)

SEXUAL ABUSE, RUNNING AWAY AND PROSTITUTION

Many young runaways have been sexually abused. McCormack *et al.* (1986) in their study of gender differences in the sexual victimisation of runaway youths found that 73% of young women and 38% of young men had been sexually abused. They contrasted this figure with the findings of a poll conducted by the *Los Angeles Times* in 1985 which indicated that 27% of women and 16% of men in the population at large had been subject to child sexual abuse. Pitts (1992) found that 17.2% of the 1152 10- to 17-year-old first admissions to the London safe house had been sexually abused. The pressures upon families in the neighbourhoods from which young people are most likely to run result in heightened levels of recorded child abuse and receptions into local authority care (Segal, 1990; Allin *et al.*, 1991; Messerschmidt, 1993). These same pressures may also precipitate family breakdown and the formation of new partnerships which can, as Kufeldt (1991) suggests, 'increase the risk of sexual abuse by a step-parent or unrelated care-giver in the home'. A study undertaken by Russell in San Francisco (1986) showed that step-daughters are seven times more likely to be sexually abused than daughters living with their biological fathers. As we have seen, Graham and Bowling (1995) found that young people are more likely to run from reconstituted and single-parent families, while the Centrepoint survey found that whereas only 50% of young people admitted to the Centrepoint projects had ever lived with both parents, 15% had lived with a step-parent and 35% had lived with one parent (Kirby, 1995). It is also evident that the majority of the young people who are in the care of, or accommodated by, local authorities have been violently or sexually abused and that those who run from care are even more likely to have been so abused (Ball *et al.*, 1991; McCormack *et al.*, 1986).

In their study of 200 prostitutes in San Francisco, Silbert and Pines (1981) discovered that 60% had been sexually abused as juveniles. The overwhelming majority of these said that they 'felt terrible' about the abuse and over 90% attributed their involvement in prostitution to it. As to the link between running away and prostitution, Yates *et al.* (1988) found that whereas only 2% of non-runaways reported involvement in prostitution, 26% of runaways reported such involvement.

DRIFTING INTO PROSTITUTION

These young people are disadvantaged in two related ways. On the one hand they have usually received a poor education, they have few marketable skills, they are casualties of family conflict, and they are homeless and impoverished. That such factors have a powerful impact upon a young person's involvement in prostitution is evidenced by the fact that the most notorious pick-up point for young male prostitutes is the pub directly across the road from London's largest nightshelter for homeless young people. On the other hand, however, unlike many of their similarly disadvantaged contemporaries, these young people also often lack relationships of kinship or friendship rooted in a geographical place, and the networks of relatives, friends or other adults who can introduce them to legitimate occupational or educational opportunities or serve as a source of support and solace where otherwise there are none.

It is not simply that their initial disadvantages propel them into prostitution, it is that those relationships and networks which might ordinarily serve to prevent their drift into self-destructive or self-defeating behaviour are absent and, to that extent, they are socially isolated. Thus, these young people have little to bind them to the conventional order and so their journey to the threshold of prostitution is unimpeded.

Nonetheless, the final impetus towards involvement in prostitution, according to McMullen (1987), is often rooted in the damage to identity and sense of self-esteem occasioned by the experience of childhood sexual abuse. He argues that young people engaged in prostitution usually have 'a poorly experienced and under-developed sense of personal power', which is the result of a combination of profound economic need, sexual abuse and exploitation, and estrangement from family and friends. He writes:

> The latter condition [the experience of abuse] is insufficiently
> motivating for children and young people. However, when linked with
> the former condition [damaged self-identity], it operates as a
> legitimating force, behind which the former condition may hide.

Thus, young people who experience themselves as having little value and virtually nothing left to lose, confront a financial situation which appears to offer them virtually no alternative.

However, the transition from non-participation to participation in prostitution requires a rationale and a reinterpretation of events if the young person is to remain on tolerable terms with themselves and to preserve a psychologically viable identity. Such a transition is achieved through the deployment of what Sykes and Matza (1957) have called 'techniques of neutralisation' in which:

> Disapproval flowing from internalised norms and conforming others in
> the social environment is neutralised, turned back or deflected in
> advance. Social controls that serve to inhibit deviant motivational
> patterns are rendered inoperative and the individual is freed to engage
> in delinquency without serious damage to the self-image. In this sense,
> the delinquent both has his cake and eats it too, for he remains
> committed to the dominant normative system and yet so qualifies its
> imperatives that violations are acceptable if not 'right'.

The techniques of neutralisation, which serve to loosen the moral bind, are derived in part from personal experience. Thus, in Silbert and Pine's study (1981), respondents said things like, 'My father bought me so who cares who else does' and, 'My brother could do it, why not everybody else? – might as well make them pay for it'. Others are learnt on the street in the company of other, similarly situated young people. Here they elaborate a world inhabited by 'punters', 'tricks', 'business girls', 'rent boys', 'hustlers', but seldom, if ever, 'prostitutes'. Because, after all, they are not really 'prostitutes'; they are 'only doing it for the money'. However, McMullen maintains that, for these 'powerless' young people, while the need for money may shape their initial commitment to prostitution, it is the momentary power that they are able to exercise over a potentially dangerous 'punter' which holds them there. These dangers, as McMullen suggests, include:

> ... the risk of rape, torture, slavery, pornography, every form of sexually transmitted disease including AIDS, violence and drug abuse to name but a few. Young people may 'deny' these risks are real in order to survive their encounters with punters. The truth is obvious: the 'denial' puts them more at risk.

Nonetheless, in these situations they are able to shake off the mood of fatalism which dogs them and experience themselves as active agents, controlling events in the world (Matza, 1964). It is for this reason that it is often the most 'streetwise' young people who, in an attempt to reclaim a plausible identity, put themselves into the most dangerous situations. The need for the 'buzz' of power and control amongst this powerless group not only outweighs, but is enhanced immensely by, the danger.

POLICING CHILD PROSTITUTION

As we have seen, contemporary policing of prostitution is still shaped by the imperatives established by the Wolfenden Report (1957) and enshrined in the Street Offences Act 1959. The attempt to get prostitution off the streets has gained greater impetus in the recent past as citizen groups have applied pressure on the police to 'clean up' their neighbourhoods. This has often been a successful strategy from the point of view of residents and the police but, as Lee and O'Brien (1995) have argued, this can simply displace the young people involved in prostitution to another area and this may:

> ... increase the risks they face as their regular 'safe' clients, and the informal support and warning networks that operate on the street are lost. Another effect of this approach may be to push more young people into the sectors of the sex industry that take place away from the public

gaze, for example, child pornography, peep shows, massage parlours and escort agencies. Even less is known about these areas of child exploitation in which children and young people are more isolated and at greater risk of coercion.

The number of cautions and prosecutions of young men and women under 18 for offences related to prostitution declined between 1989 and 1993, even though the actual numbers of young people involved in prostitution are believed to have increased over the period. Lee and O'Brien attribute this, in part, to the *de facto* creation of 'tolerance zones' in many UK cities, in which the police, in effect, manage rather than prosecute prostitution. The problem with such 'tolerance' is that, within these zones, the duty of the police to 'protect' children and young people falls into abeyance.

Making choices

In an attempt to avoid stigmatising young people involved in prostitution, some commentators have chosen to describe them as 'workers in the sex industry'. This euphemism, though kindly meant, merely serves to obscure the enormity of the violation. It suggests that their work is freely chosen whereas it is better seen as powerfully determined by negative experiences and reduced circumstances which constrain young people to act in ways which are inimical to their best interests. In such circumstances, as McMullen (1987) argues, it becomes somewhat irrelevant to concern ourselves, as some commentators have, with legalistic arguments about the age of consent, the precise moment at which a young person should be free to assume full responsibility for, and exercise a choice about, their sexual behaviour. Such concerns divert us from the far more complex and important question of the 'conditions of assent', the circumstances under which such consent is given. This, in turn, leads us to a consideration of the social, economic and personal circumstances under which those young people who find themselves involved in the highly dangerous business of prostitution would be able to articulate their predicament and make positive, informed choices about their lives.

The decline of the public sphere

As we have noted, the question of the origin and nature of child and youth prostitution in the UK has been neglected by governments. As a result, the children and young people who are involved in prostitution are treated, to all intents and purposes, as if they were adults. This has meant that, in the spirit of Wolfenden, policy makers and the police have been more concerned with the affront these young people present to public decency than the threat their involvement in this dangerous occupation poses to their wellbeing.

We have also seen that neighbourhood decline, poverty, poor education, unemployment, homelessness, social isolation and sexual abuse are closely associated with involvement in youth prostitution and that young people who are involved in it will tend to engage in other potentially dangerous behaviours like heavy drinking, the use of narcotics and, sometimes, suicide attempts. However, the social predicament of the young people involved in prostitution is similar, and derives from a similar source, as that encountered by other young people who are in local authority care, living in troubled families, homeless, living on the streets, unemployed, addicted, involved in persistent offending or excluded from school.

It is also the case that the period since 1979 has seen a substantial increase in the numbers of young people in most of these categories. This rise has been paralleled by a reduction in residential accommodation and housing for young people, a marked reduction in their state benefit entitlements, the contraction of public services and state resources in general, and those for troubled young people in particular. Thus, we have seen the virtual disappearance of such dedicated local authority youth social work services as existed in favour of an offence-focused youth justice service. Those parts of the voluntary sector which have been annexed by youth justice, probation and, more recently, Michael Howard's new Secure Training Centres, to enable the government to achieve its law and order objectives, have by contrast prospered. But other areas of the voluntary sector have seen dramatic reductions in state support and many voluntary youth agencies have closed. The youth service has been allowed to wither on the branch through lack of investment and now, in some areas, it is effectively nonexistent. The squeeze on state education has meant that pastoral services become harder and harder to defend when school governors are faced with making classroom teachers redundant. For its part, the education welfare service has been driven back to its original 'school board' role of the surveillance and prosecution of truants and their parents.

MARKET SOCIETY AND THE DECLINE OF CITIZENSHIP

It is not simply that there is greater need and fewer organisations and individuals available to respond to that need, however. The nature of public services and of the 'public' itself has changed over recent years. Currie (1991) has argued that the advent of what he calls 'market society' has been a major factor in the growth of problems amongst young people and the capacity of citizens in neighbourhoods to cope with these problems. He writes:

> By market society I mean a society in which the pursuit of private gain increasingly becomes the organising principle for all areas of social life, not simply a mechanism which we use to accomplish certain circumscribed economic ends. The balance between private and public shifts dramatically, so that the public retreats to a minuscule and disempowered part of social and economic life and the idea of common purposes and common responsibilities steadily withers as an important social value.

Currie maintains that market society, because it promotes inequality and economic deprivation, weakens the capacity of communities and families to support or control their young people. It also reduces 'publics', a collectivity of citizens and as such, a political entity, to 'markets' composed of individuals who are 'empowered', if they have a pound, by the pound in their pocket. This transformation means that the public sphere is, in effect, 'depoliticised'. In the UK, this depoliticisation has been achieved by the progressive concentration in the hands of central government of powers previously invested in local government and alongside this the privatisation and marketisation of public services. But these new quasi-markets represented by the new slimline, 'customer-oriented' managerially 'driven' public services, like real markets, are attuned only to the 'effective demand' of 'purchasers' rather than the hopes, aspirations and fears of publics. Being disconnected from local publics, local politics and local problems, public services can no longer be the means whereby private troubles are translated into public issues (Mills, 1957). Thus, alongside the loss of a service is a *de facto* disenfranchisement in which an important connection between publics and the political process has been severed at local level.

NEW FORMS OF SOLIDARITY

This political isolation is particularly worrying at a time when family forms and traditional social relationships in neighbourhoods in decline are being eroded by a rising divorce rate and rapid population change which is, in turn, one feature of global economic change. Arguably, it is precisely during such periods of social, cultural and economic change that the voices of those rendered most vulnerable by these changes should be heard. In the European Community (EC) this problem of political articulation from below has been identified as part of the broader problem of 'social exclusion' and the erosion of traditional forms of family and neighbourhood solidarity (Delors, 1993).

One attempted solution, pioneered in France in the 1980s as part of François Mitterand's Politique de la Ville, lies in the construction and support of new forms of social solidarity based on the development of democratic participation in decision-making by young people at neighbourhood level (Pitts, 1995). Unlike the traditional forms of solidarity which they replace, they are not bounded by the workplace and membership of trades unions and political parties. Within these structures, young people participate in decisions about housing, the development of social services, education, training and employment in the neighbourhoods in which they live. In doing so, they have formal access to local professionals and politicians to whom they are able to explain problems and with whom they can discuss their preferred solutions. In some neighbourhoods, this has led to the development of housing which enables extended families to live in close proximity and local, professionally supported 'foyers' in which young people who are unable to live at home can nonetheless retain links with their other social networks. It has also led to the initiation of long-term, neighbourhood-based, vocational training which aims to progressively upgrade young people's skills and qualifications to the point where they are able to compete for permanent skilled and semi-skilled roles in the local economy.

In a similar vein, the 1994 EC conference on the family in Europe in the year 2000 (German Ministry for the Family, 1995) commended a broader view of the family as an evolving and increasingly complex set of relationships which must be supported by the state in order to maximise its positive potential to enhance the chances and choices of children. The notion of a partnership between central and local government and these new families to further the interests of children is, by contemporary UK standards, a remarkably radical one.

In his analysis of the problems of young people in the USA, Currie (1991) comes to very similar conclusions. He argues that at a macro level we need a 'solidaristic' 'active labour market' policy of the type pursued in Scandinavian countries, which aims to provide dignified public sector work which develops skills and opens up new opportunities for socially excluded young people. He points to social democratic tax and benefit policies which aim to reduce discrepancies of wealth, not least because such discrepancies generate massively expensive problems of crime, social order and welfare dependency. The third plank of his programme concerns an 'active family policy': a comprehensive package of child and family interventions which prevent child abuse by supporting families to cope with 'real world' stress in their neighbourhoods; provide high quality pre-school education; and a comprehensive youth strategy which offers 'changed lives' and extended possibilities for young people, and a move from a 'deficiency' to an 'opportunity' model of work with them.

Like the Delors Report (1993), Currie identifies the central problem as the 'running down' of modern economies with a consequent shrinkage of opportunities for young people to use their talent and ability. For Currie, these initiatives are all part of the construction of citizenship, ways of giving young people a stake in conformity and a stake in society.

Such a programme is needed urgently, he believes, because the USA and Britain appear to be teetering on the edge of a state of 'economic apartheid' in which most youth crime, addiction, prostitution, etc. will be concentrated in a permanently excluded, impoverished outgroup. What this means politically, he says, is that the prevention of social ills:

> ... is now more than ever dependent on our capacity to build more effective movements for social action and social change. These movements should challenge effectively those forces dimming the life-chances of vast numbers of people in the developed and developing worlds. Building organisations should be committed to the long-range effort to replace a society based increasingly on the least inspiring human values with one based on the principles of social solidarity and contributive justice.

YOUTH PROSTITUTION IN A STAKEHOLDER SOCIETY

How do these American and mainland European analyses and innovations sit within the 'stakeholder society', an ideological underpinning which is now preferred by the Labour Party. Clearly, the recent 'tough' pronouncements by New Labour and Mandelson and Liddle (1996) about the behaviour of young people aim to wrest the mantle of 'law and order' from the Conservatives. More importantly, however, they indicate that at present, like the Conservatives, Labour is unwilling to fashion policies which address the profound social and economic changes which have occurred in the UK since the 1970s. It appears that Labour is opting for new forms of discipline, rather than new forms of solidarity, in order to engender feelings of security and confidence in the 'stake-holders'. But what does New Labour have to offer young people who have no such stake in the future?

The Mitterand administrations of the 1980s believed that with the restructuring of the world economy since the 1960s and the advent of structural youth unemployment, a new politics was needed if social cohesion was to be maintained. The Politique de la Ville was an initiative geared to the stark realities of a changed and changing world which was seen to have generated a 'crisis in citizenship'. In practice, therefore, Mitterand's initiative strove to turn young people with no stake in conformity into 'stakeholders' through the elaboration of new forms of solidarity, new modes of democratic participation, and the collaborative development of new educational and vocational opportunities for 'socially excluded' young people.

For New Labour, such a move would require a radical shift of perspective from one which appears to regard socially excluded young people as a parasitic and potentially predatory residual population, lurking menacingly on the periphery of civil society, to one which views them as a constituency of citizens with their own needs and their own unique contribution, who should be at the centre of their neighbourhoods, the centre of their society and, by extension, the centre of their own lives.

But if something like this were to be possible, if we could establish these links, if we could allow these young people some power and control in determining how their lives might unfold; if they, in partnership with professionals and politicians, were able to specify the most effective responses to their needs and their hopes, but also the distinctive contribution they could make, we would have moved a long way towards an engagement with the factors which culminate in youth prostitution and the other, related, problems discussed in this chapter.

Conclusion: Where from here?

David Barrett

Events involving the abuse and degradation of children seemed to reach new levels of depravity in the months that this book was being prepared. In North West Europe alone there was the Dunblane massacre, the aftermath of the Wests' trial and the discovery of the Belgian paedophile ring. Further afield, globalisation means that markets, travel and new technology are all contributors to the continued expansion of child sex tourism.

Closer to home, but just as relentless, has been the continued rise in the number of children living in poverty. In 1979, 1.4 million children were living in poverty, defined as household income of less than the national average income after housing costs. By 1992–93 this had increased to 4.3 million – one in three children in the UK (Department of Social Security, 1995). Many of these children exist in impoverished neighbourhoods; these are not only in inner cities, but also in some shire county towns and small non-urban locations. Some of these children are involved in child prostitution.

Now, even identifying the locations where children operate as prostitutes, as the media frequently does, has recently created a new phenomenon whereby a location is identified, the punters (to use the vernacular) are attracted to the area, demand cannot be met and then more prostitutes (and usually pimps) target the area too. What could have been a manageable problem suddenly becomes out of control.

MAKING SENSE OF WHAT THE CONTRIBUTORS HAVE SAID

The contributions in this book outline many ideas and practical responses and identify many sad episodes and scenarios. However, they also bring thoughts and proposals that will be helpful to others, therefore both hope and optimism are apparent. As well as their specialist input, contributors were also asked to consider questions of oppression such as race, class, disability and gender; some interesting insights are proffered here.

Two observations need to be made. Firstly, readers will note that none of the contributors is from a social services department. The editor and publisher approached and worked with a senior manager for many months, a draft was submitted but ultimately permission to publish the contribution was not granted. As the other contributors convey, social services' work with children involved in prostitution has in the past been found wanting – these issues are developed later in this chapter. Secondly, there is not a separate contribution from a probation service based worker: the service's diminishing preventative work with younger people is simply a sign of the times, but it is acknowledged that the service supports some work in this area.

We have attempted to synthesise the main points from the contributions to the book from various angles which are set out below. This is followed by some recommendations. These are particularly timely as the Department of Health is currently reviewing its 'Working Together' guidelines issued to those involved in child protection – it is our intention that this book will influence that review.

PRACTITIONERS' WORK WITH CHILD PROSTITUTES

All of the chapters from practitioners who work with children involved in prostitution consistently identify three points that are relevant to the examination of child prostitution. They are precipitating factors, relevant issues and practice insights and ideas. After these three areas are explored, the most common themes are identified and some analysis of them takes place.

Precipitating factors

What circumstances and factors contribute to children being involved in prostitution? Trafford and Hayes in their contribution talk about the 'push' and 'pull' factors that influence those young people on the street: conditions at home that may push people to run away or move on; and pull factors from the street that may glamorise such a lifestyle, and lead the children to ignore the harsh realities of some aspects of the life such as the manipulative abilities of pimps. A typology of young people involved in prostitution has begun to emerge based on backgrounds that are very disadvantaged.

What can be seen consistently, however, from the contributors is that children at various junctures on their journey to adulthood suffer many forms of oppression. The push/pull factors are examples of this. Others include the link Pitts has made between poverty and abuse. He discusses the effects on some young people of living in neighbourhoods that are in decline, and their drift into self-destructive behaviour which is unlikely to be impeded once it has started. Bowen argues that school exclusions add to the chances of young people being caught in a cycle of drift and aimless and pointless lifestyles, a point made powerfully elsewhere (Brodie and Berridge, 1996). One aspect of the English Collective of Prostitutes (ECP) chapter argues that young people involved in child prostitution are living their lives where only 'bad choices' are available and that any choice that is exercised is often the lesser of two evils. Meanwhile, a change in the value base and language of welfare provision to one of targets and business plans has impeded social services' ability to provide good quality services for young people.

Strain within the family has also been given prominence by several of our contributors, not least Louise. Economic shortfall has been given particular attention here, receiving comment from Bowen and Pitts. Green *et al.* and Pitts both make the observation that changes in legislation that relate to benefit levels and housing opportunities have been unhelpful for the welfare of people generally, and young people in particular. Other features that may contribute to strain include poor housing, unemployment and diminishing welfare support. Faugier and Sargeant suggest that these additional strains within families can lead to family breakdown and are contributory factors to young people running away from the family and exposing themselves to the dangers of street cultures. These actions often have serious consequences for the health of the children concerned.

The perpetrators (i.e. the punters/abusers) involved in child prostitution have various involvements as the ECP, Edgington, Aitchison and O'Brien, and Louise's examples demonstrate. There is increasing evidence to link childhood sexual abuse with prostitution: low self-esteem, looking for an escape route, being in a position to exercise some power are cited. Therefore, a perpetrator within a family may cause the young person to flee the family home to be exploited by other perpetrators. Although unusual, even some parents 'work' their children as prostitutes. Pimps are particularly skilled at identifying vulnerable young people and filling emotional and physical voids in their lives – but they abuse young people sexually, emotionally and physically. The other main perpetrators involved are the punters themselves. More recently, it has become more commonly accepted that punters are not 'overt' monsters or ogres but are 'ordinary' men going about their daily business who are willing to pay an extra premium for sex with children.

The law as it relates to prostitution generally, and to child prostitution in particular, is complex. Aitchison and O'Brien identify some of the finer points of the criminal and civil law in relation to child prostitution. Probably the most contentious aspect surrounding the law is its application, or lack of it. As has been demonstrated by Aitchison and O'Brien, and Edgington, the application can be selective, highly variable and inconsistent. But for the children involved in child prostitution the law is very clear: the Children Act 1989 caters for such children at risk, on a 'partnership' basis. The criminal law is also clear about where it stands on the perpetrators, but again the application is often left wanting. Adult prostitution often receives a neutral response from agencies involved in dealing with it. This same neutrality appears to generate a similar passivity when children are involved. There are examples too of children being pursued inappropriately by the criminal law (Lee and O'Brien, 1995).

This apparent lack of commitment to deal with child prostitution by some of the relevant agencies, most of whom are represented in this book, is mystifying. Young prostitutes are a difficult group to work with but the task is not insurmountable as The Children's Society and Barnardo's, to name but two agencies involved in this work, consistently demonstrate. The Area Child Protection Committees (ACPCs) have a multi-disciplinary and legal mandate via social services to deal with children who are in need of protection. This includes their Children's Service Planning role, and Looking After Children responsibilities. It can be argued that these tasks are too important to be left to the discretion of locally based planning and implementation. However, ACPCs are ideally placed to lead on the issue and to intervene accordingly. Their reluctance to become involved is now, and perhaps rather belatedly, possibly about to change (see below).

Relevant issues

It is apparent from the contributions that certain key factors that play a central role in propelling children into prostitution can be identified. The contributions also, however, beg a number of questions.

Where does the issue of child prostitution sit? Is it a moral, educational, judicial or health issue? It is all of these and many more too. Despite the strong arguments that the issue of, and thus the response to, child prostitution is one of 'welfare' not 'justice', central government, up until the summer of 1996, had yet to hear that message (see also Lee and O'Brien, 1995).

However, 1996 became something of a watershed for young people and prostitution. Events at home included a series of children's charities reports on the subject, continuing media attention and the usual display of local authority ambivalence. A significant event took place abroad – the Stockholm Conference (The World Congress against Commercial Sexual Exploitation of Children organised jointly by UNICEF and ECPAT). It highlighted the plight globally of children being exploited sexually, including through prostitution. These events at home and abroad eventually served to concentrate the government's mind on the area of child sexual exploitation.

The Home Office responded somewhat hastily to the Stockholm Conference (Home Office, 1996) but with minimal input from the Department for Education and Employment (DfEE), and the Department of Health (DoH), producing a response that has national and international implications. The Home Office report attempts to do many things simultaneously, including promises of extra-territorial legislation and extra police effort. However, there is no new commitment to the children involved in prostitution on the streets in the UK now. It is difficult not to interpret the Home Office action as politically inspired, independent from the DoH which should be leading on this issue in the UK on behalf of child welfare.

Perhaps most fundamentally, social policy changes over the last few years and central government's regressive attitude towards welfare in general have combined to militate against 'children in need'. Even the government's Children Act 1989, hailed as an enlightened and creative piece of legislation at the time, based on the 'partnership' concept, is now falling foul of wide variations in implementation and interpretation. Children 'in need' sometimes become 'children at risk' in danger of 'significant harm'. Although not originally drafted to deal with children involved in street culture (children on the street were largely absent in the mid 1980s), the wording of the Act is flexible enough to include children involved in prostitution. Aitchison and O'Brien powerfully remind local authorities of their duties here.

Recently, inadequate social policy, or non-implementation, has been connected very directly to child prostitution as *The Game's Up* (1995), *Splintered Lives* (1995), Barnardo's Bradford Street And Lanes Project (Barnardo's, 1996) all demonstrate. Several contributors to this book support such an analysis (cf. Pitts, Edgington, and Green *et al.*). An erosion of the commitment to a welfare response for young street people does appear to be taking place. The experiences of children who have left local authority care are a clear example of this because follow-up services for these people are virtually nonexistent.

Violence, invisibility, denial, harassment, ghettoisation, health risks (mental and physical), these are some of the ingredients of child prostitution as the ECP, and Faugier and Sargeant note. Existing in a brothel or an off-street sex parlour in a sink neighbourhood, under the control of a pimp who has probably made the child drug dependent, where physical violence is commonplace, is virtually impossible for an unsupported young person to escape from. Residents from such neighbourhoods are inadequately helped by professionals, who, unsurprisingly get frightened too as Faugier and Sargeant argue. These depressed areas are rarely policed effectively and the culture of pimps and prostitutes is often ignored. Understandably, young people involved in prostitution in such areas, with the stigma that goes with it, do not envisage a future which is worth seeking.

Families who live in such neighbourhoods also suffer additional pressures, some of which are alluded to above. The effects on mental health of such an existence are becoming more widely accepted, as Faugier and Sargeant suggest. Edgington points out somewhat delicately that some areas receive a higher policing presence than others, suggesting that the policing of 'red-light' districts is not always a priority. In some other areas, however, as the ECP observe, there are police targeting operations. One of the effects of this can be that young people are hassled off their patch and into a new area, where none of the informal support systems operate (Trafford and Hayes).

Selective attention and implementation of both civil and criminal law appears to be quite common practice in relation to child prostitution. Some areas of the country seem to pursue the civil route, as Trafford and Hayes identify. Other areas follow the criminal law route, but generally the policing of prostitution is not a top policing priority for chief officers, as Edgington observes. It appears to be an either/or scenario, the civil or criminal; in the latter case the protection of children is frequently ignored. Therefore, the service some young people receive can be heavily dependent on geography. This overall lack of co-ordination of services seems a key element and one that Green *et al.* make most strongly. They argue that an adequately funded youth service could play a pivotal role here, particularly in relation to understanding and accessing street cultures. Additional and supportive actions by lawyers (Aitchison and

O'Brien) and teachers (Bowen), are also propounded. We must remember that Louise's experience was not one of the services not being present, but one of them not hearing and believing her, therefore they were not able to be activated.

When children run away from their homes, they are often entering a new world of exploitation. In some cases there will be perpetrators of offences both where they ran from and where they ran to. This is an invidious position for the child to be in and also for the unknowing or unbelieving professional. But what we do know is that life for the young prostitute is very dangerous, which many of those with such experience know to their cost. We also know that some families have not provided their children with the necessary structure and controls to enable the children to value themselves. This is not surprising following a recent DoH report *Focus on Teenagers* (1996b) which acknowledges that generally work with teenagers, and support for it, requires more recognition. But surely there are shortcomings in a society (Kroll and Barrett, 1995) where a Prime Minister encourages us to '... condemn a little more and understand a little less'. (*Mail on Sunday*, 21 February, 1993).

Practice insights and ideas

As the material in the introduction to the book has identified elsewhere, there have already been experiences of professionals working with children involved in prostitution and several possible approaches have been identified, for example, those by Green, Jesson and Lee and O'Brien. However, in the most recent past, several other projects have written up their work (for example, Barnardo's Streets And Lanes Project (SALs)) or research teams have reported (Shaw *et al.*, 1996; Shaw and Butler, forthcoming). Others have prepared material for the Stockholm Conference (for example, Warburton and Camacho de la Cruz). Here is not the place to revisit all of that material but some of it will be referred to. The contributors to this book have identified their respective insights, ideas and models too.

For example, Aitchison and O'Brien argue here most strongly for an approach when working with young people involved in prostitution that places emphasis on criminalising those who exploit the children, categorising them as abusers rather than criminalising the young people themselves. This point is given similar prominence by the SALs Project and Shaw and Butler in their discussion about an integrated approach to a delivery of services to young people involved in prostitution. This integration includes strategic and reflective planning and implementation across a range of statutory and non-statutory services that are a part of a wider commitment to young people.

How can we transfer some of these insights into effective work with abused children involved in prostitution? The contributors here have many helpful suggestions. In undertaking outreach streetwork, of which there are several different models, Trafford and Hayes develop their own model from practice experience. They outline the importance of staff safety, identify some strategies to employ and also highlight the importance of confidentiality and equal opportunities in streetwork practice. Integration of services also appears to be crucial since piecemeal approaches appear to fail. The importance of education, the youth service, social services and health working together is emphasised by Green *et al.* and Bowen. This approach could be utilised within the school programme and curriculum, including the building of self-esteem for relevant pupils (Bowen). Referral pathways for help such as counselling are also difficult to identify (Edgington) and elements of compulsion for any such pathways inhibit voluntary involvement. It has to be recognised that there are also dilemmas when compulsion is proposed, for example, the use of secure accommodation may affect a young person adversely in many ways.

Child prostitution appears in practice to be on the periphery of the child protection system, and sometimes estranged from it, but Bowen reminds us that issues such as bullying have been brought from fringe to the mainstream, utilising the concept of 'survivors' rather than victims. Although some organisations compensate for the shortfalls of local authorities and the paucity of services, co-ordination is of paramount importance (Aitchison and O'Brien, the ECP, Faugier and Sargeant, Pitts). The importance of strategic planning cannot be overplayed. It also reinforces how well placed ACPCs are to develop preventative initiatives and comprehensive inter-agency services to support the child protection process. Referrals from one agency to another can be problematic as Louise's experience demonstrated and while Faugier and Sargeant outline the advantages of 'fast-track' referrals, they also identify the shortcomings of such an approach in that it maintains the service as both different and peripheral.

COMMON THEMES

The Council of Europe (1993) helpfully reminds us that the emphasis should be placed on children as victims of sexual exploitation and not as perpetrators of or accomplices to criminal offences. This usefully establishes a value base for identifying common themes. Previously, Lee and O'Brien (1995) reminded us about the power of language and that when talking of 'young prostitutes' we are talking about children who are abused. O'Brien, this time with Aitchison, reinforces the point again here with the support of the SALs Project. Bowen, Green *et al.*, and Faugier and Sargeant all discuss the importance of education and preventative services. Since any such services need to be part of a wider commitment to young people who are forced into street life, these services too should also be mainstream and not peripheral.

The powerlessness of the children involved and the way they have been discriminated against is present in every contributor's work; whether it is poverty, health risks or services letting children down, they all amount to children in need being excluded from what is rightfully theirs. Where some argue that some young people 'choose' prostitution, we have to ask ourselves what other 'choices' they had at their disposal.

It is clear that families can be both instigators of the route into prostitution for children but also a safe place for them to return to. Abusers of children are notoriously reluctant to admit their crimes. The main perpetrators sometimes reside within the family and sometimes outside; the evidence here suggests that for those children involved in prostitution the initial abuse has normally occurred within the family. The pre-sexualising of children cannot be readily reversed.

Decriminalisation of the children involved in prostitution, increasing the tariff for those caught abusing children and the consistent implementation and application of both the civil law (for the children) and the criminal law (for the perpetrators) has been consistently argued for.

The call for integrated services and a spirit of partnership between them has also been to the fore, with more leadership required from central government on the issues involved. A framework exists for action (i.e. ACPCs) but more impetus is required. The pioneering track record of the children's charities in this area has much it can teach local and national government.

RECOMMENDATIONS

In some ways it is quite easy to produce another abstract list of recommendations that is dislocated from the everyday rigours and realities of service providers. However, the consistency between the recommendations below and those that have previously been argued for elsewhere should sound alarm bells for decision-makers. Some messages have been given time and time again and will doubtless continue to be conveyed until they are heard and acted upon – some are aims and objectives which should be pursued, others are urgent demands for change, others suggest the means whereby such changes may be brought about. We have erred on the side of brevity. We were going to suggest a timetable of implementation but with a general election imminent at the time of writing those of the recommendations that require changes in the law may, in the short term, fall on deaf ears. However, young people involved in what, hitherto, we have termed child prostitution, need access to informed and universal services with specialist knowledge and the staff to offer such a service. It has been argued consistently through the work of most contributors here that the system for this is already in place across the country via the ACPCs.

Of the specific recommendations, the first four concern legal matters, the next two relate to education and the remainder concern central government; they include some new ideas and initiatives:

- Local authority services must not be selective in the exercise of their statutory duties under the civil law and the existing system of ACPCs can be utilised, not least because it is an exemplar of multi-agency working.

- The Sexual Offences Acts need to be amended so as to be consistent with the Children Act 1989, and police services and the Crown Prosecution Service must not be selective with the implementation of their mandatory obligations under the criminal law.

- The criminal law should not be utilised to criminalise these children and the using of children as prostitutes should be redefined as child abuse, with sentencing tariffs employed accordingly. Within this, cognisance should be taken of the spirit of the UN Convention and the Council of Europe regarding child sexual exploitation.

- The statutory responsibility of local authorities' post-care obligations for young people leaving care should be implemented more rigorously.

- Education and training should target 'helping professionals' who work with abused children in order that professionals may more effectively mobilise the services that already exist for young people.

- Education Departments should be more proactive with sex education and health issues on the curriculum, and recognise more fully their statutory role in child protection as it concerns youngsters on the edge of or involved in child prostitution.

- Government Departments, including any new initiatives, should be co-ordinated by the DoH, the lead agency on child welfare and child abuse, as a positive role model for all the services involved.

- Extreme social inequalities should be compensated for by targeted benefits so as to prevent children entering prostitution for economic reasons.

- Central government, health, welfare and education agencies must recognise the contribution of economic and neighbourhood destabili-sation to family breakdown, running away and child prostitution.

- Urgent consideration should be given to the establishment of a net-work of safe accommodation, including Foyers in which vulnerable young people could be accommodated, into their early twenties if necessary, to be commissioned by central government and run and co-ordinated by the children's charities.

Most of the above require little if any extra resources, but rather a shift in emphasis and an expression of political will. If central government is reluctant to ask local authorities to address these issues, it may find it more politically acceptable to purchase such a national service to deal with child abuse from a major children's charity or some of them working together. This may focus the minds of all the players concerned. The usual delays will no doubt occur but the abuse will continue, the children will still be waiting.

Some useful initiatives

More optimistically, in the summer of 1996, communication between some of the key players involved in dealing with children involved in prostitution took place. Professional responses to child prostitution in Britain 'are being reviewed', announced the Association of Chief Police Officers (ACPO), the Association of Directors of Social Services (ADSS) and The Children's Society in a joint press statement (22 August, 1996). The review of police practice in dealing with children involved in prostitution is to place more emphasis on the protection of the children and the prosecution of the adults who abuse or profit from exploiting them.

ACPO also set up a working group on the issue which includes representation from the DoH, the ADSS, The Children's Society, the Crown Prosecution Service and the Home Office (at the time of going to press this
initiative was being joined by other players).

· Research has a role to play too. Although some small-scale research
has been undertaken, as has been noted in the introduction to the book,
a national overview has yet to be undertaken. Even though this will be a
methodologically complex piece of work, it is nevertheless vitally necessary if we are to make a realistic response to the problem in the long
term. But this lack of data should not hinder immediate action. We know
we have a problem. We know some of the causes of why children enter
prostitution, we also know the effects and consequences.

Have the aims of the book been achieved?

We have presented a collection of chapters on practice issues in child
prostitution. For the first time, a range of perspectives covering key professional groups and agencies who work in the area has been given. It
was our intention to move the professional debate about how to respond
to child prostitution forward.

The embarrassment that child prostitution brings is considerable.
Attention on children involved in prostitution defines sharply the
number of years the government has avoided the issue. Does the government want a legacy of creating a children's social policy environment
that will be known as one that legitimised the existence of street children in this country? The pictures of these children now are reminiscent
of those that many of the children's charities have of street children in
their archives taken in the last century.

We cannot leave the children's charities to continually fill the gap
left by the shortcomings of local authorities and central government.
Surely in a sane world they would complement state provision, creating
pioneering and innovative alternatives, not, as is now the case, competing with it and struggling to make good its deficits.

In his annual report for 1995, the Chief Inspector of the Social
Services Inspectorate, Sir Herbert Laming, was blunt when commenting
about the delivery of children's services. He said that we have been
dominated by an overly pathological model which looks at how things
have gone wrong. A move is required to do things with people, not for
people, he argues.

The political uncertainty concerning the future of welfare may be less relevant now. As *The Economist* somewhat acerbically notes, different political futures of welfare are difficult to predict: 'the difference between these competing versions of the welfare state are puny' (21 September, 1996). It is in this climate that we are looking forward. But nevertheless, we look forward to improving our practice, working with individuals, families, communities, and neighbourhoods.

The involvement of young people in prostitution will not disappear imminently – we are realists too! However, we hope that this book contributes to the development of effective interventions with young people involved in prostitution. To this end the book has moved beyond mere ideas – it brings together examples of how working with child prostitutes can be accomplished.

Let us not forget the many powerful messages that Louise gave us at the beginning of the book. 'If someone had been there for me, if someone had listened to me ... I may have been something else'. We all know that prostitution is a behaviour and does not define a person. What a relief it was for Louise when a residential social worker finally listened and 'heard' what she was saying – she was finally believed. Her courage 'to tell' earlier in her life had been betrayed. Her journey into prostitution had been taking place over a period of time, and like other youngsters involved in child prostitution, the route, while apparently inexorable, could well have been changed.

Observing and evaluating how services work, or do not work, has been an ever increasing necessity in an era when quality assurance has properly taken root in the area of welfare provision. The need for partnership between managers, practitioners and researchers based on a shared commitment to the improvement of practice, and the quality of service to users, has also been widely accepted (Gostick, 1991). But moving beyond partnership and collaboration in a way that 'makes a difference' is still being striven for by many – not least some child protection agencies. However difficult these seemingly modest goals are to achieve, they are worthy objectives nevertheless – we must keep trying.

Appendix 1

Table 1: Cautions and convictions against females of between the ages of 10 and 17 in England and Wales 1989 to 1995.

Age	10	11	12	13	14	15	16	17	Total
1989 Cautioned	0	0	0	3	9	32	60	268	372
Convicted	0	0	0	0	0	5	24	361	390
1990 Cautioned	0	0	2	3	13	19	99	292	428
Convicted	0	0	0	0	1	2	22	346	371
1991 Cautioned	0	0	1	5	10	34	111	200	361
Convicted	0	0	3	0	0	5	35	278	321
1992 Cautioned	1	0	1	1	6	41	62	189	301
Convicted	0	0	1	0	0	7	25	215	248
1993 Cautioned	0	0	0	5	32	32	82	145	296
Convicted	0	0	0	0	0	7	25	73	105
1994 Cautioned	0	0	1	5	19	25	96	157	303
Convicted	0	0	0	1	3	13	35	90	142
1995 Cautioned	0	0	2	4	11	27	63	156	263
Convicted	0	0	0	0	0	4	25	72	101

Table 2: Cautions and convictions against males of between the ages of 10 and 17 in England and Wales 1989 to 1995.

Age	14	15	16	17	Total
1989 Cautioned	0	0	2	11	13
Convicted	1	0	1	18	20
1990 Cautioned	1	0	3	6	10
Convicted	1	1	1	8	11
1991 Cautioned	0	1	3	1	5
Convicted	0	0	2	10	12
1992 Cautioned	2	3	2	4	11
Convicted	0	0	0	4	4
1993 Cautioned	3	0	1	2	6
Convicted	0	0	0	1	1
1994 Cautioned	1	1	2	4	8
Convicted	0	0	0	0	0
1995 Cautioned	0	1	0	2	3
Convicted	0	0	1	3	4

Source: Home Office

References

Abrahams, C., Mungall, R. (1992) *Runaways: Exploding the Myths*. London: National Children's Homes.

Advisory Council on the Misuse of Drugs (1991) *Drug Misusers and the Criminal Justice System Part 1: Community Resources and the Probation Service*. London: HMSO.

Allin, M., Barrett, D., Canham, H., Harris, G. *et al.* (1991) 'Preparation for poverty: Rethinking residential care'. J. Dennington and J. Pitts (eds.) *Developing Services for Young People in Crisis*. Harlow: Longman.

Appleton, J. V. (1996) 'Working with vulnerable families: A health visiting perspective'. *Journal of Advanced Nursing*, vol. 23, pp. 912–8.

Bagley, C. (1991) 'The long-term psychological effects of child sexual abuse: A review of some British and Canadian studies of victims and their families'. *Annals of Sex Research*, vol. 4, no. 4, pp. 23–48.

Ball, L., Chatterton, W., Clarke, M., Cullen, J. *et al.* (1991) 'Breaking the silence: Developing work with abused young people in care'. J. Dennington and J. Pitts (eds.) *Developing Services for Young People in Crisis*. Harlow: Longman.

Barnardo's (1996) Streets and Lanes (SALs) Annual Report, April 1995. London: Barnardo's.

Barnard, M., McKeganey, N., Bloor, M. (1990) 'A risky business'. *Community Care*, no. 5, July, pp. 26–7.

Barrett, D. (1994a) 'Social work on the street: Responding to juvenile prostitution in Amsterdam, London and Paris'. *Social Work in Europe*, vol. 1, no. 1, pp. 29–32.

Barrett, D. (1994b) 'Stop the bus, we want to get on'. *The Guardian*, 10 August.

Barrett, D. (1995) 'Child prostitution'. *Highlight*, no. 135. London: National Children's Bureau.

Barrett, D., Beckett, W. (1996) 'Health promoting itself: Reaching out to children who sell sex to survive'. *British Journal of Nursing*, vol. 5, no. 18, pp. 1128–5.

Barton, S., Taylor-Robinson, D., Harris, J. (1987) 'Female prostitutes and sexually transmitted diseases'. *British Journal of Hospital Medicine*, vol. 7, pp. 34–45.

Benson, C., Matthews, R. (1995) *National Vice Squad Survey*. Middlesex University.

Benson, C., Matthews, R. (1996) *Report of the Parliamentary Group on Prostitution*. Middlesex University.

Berridge, D., Cleaver, H. (1987) *Foster Home Breakdown*. Oxford: Basil Blackwell Ltd.

Biehal, N., Clayden, J., Stein, M., Wade, J. (1992) *Prepared for Living?: A Survey of Young People Leaving the Care of Three Local Authorities*. London: National Children's Bureau.

Blennerhassett, R., Gilvarry, E. (1996) 'The streetwise clinic: An integrated approach to the assessment of substance use and misuse in young people'. *Childright*, no. 127, p. 4.

Blume, S. B. (1990a) 'Alcohol and drug problems in women: Old attitudes, new knowledge'. H. B. Milkman and L. l. Sederer (eds.) *Treatment Choices for Alcoholism and Substance Abuse*. Lexington D.C: Health and Company.

Blume, S. B. (1990b) 'Chemical dependency in women: Important issues'. *American Journal of Drug and Alcohol Abuse*, vol. 16 (3 and 4), pp. 297–307.

Boyle, S. (1994) *Working Girls and their Men: Male Sexual Desires and Fantasies Revealed by the Women Paid to Satisfy Them*. London: Smith Gryphon Publishers.

Brodie, I., Berridge, D. (1996) *School Exclusion: Research Themes and Issues*. University of Luton.

Bullock, R., Millham, S. (1989) 'Managing the family contacts of children absent in care: Professional and legislative issues – the UK experience'. Paper presented to the NATO Advanced Research Workshop, Aquafredda di Maratea, Italy, 20–24 February.

Bury, J. (1990) 'Drug use in primary care'. J. Strang and G. V. Stimson (1990) *Aids and Drug Misuse: The Challenge for Policy and Practice in the 1990s*. London: Routledge.

Calcetas-Santos, O. (1996) *Rights of the Child: Report of the Special Rapporteur on the Sale of Children, Child Prostitution and Child Pornography*. Prepared for The United Nations Commission on Human Rights. Geneva: United Nations Economic and Social Contract.

Cameron, S., Peacock, W., Trotter, G. (1993) 'Reaching out'. *Nursing Times*, vol. 89, no. 7, pp. 34–6.

Carballo, M., Rezza, G. (1990) 'AIDS, drug misuse and the global crisis'. J. Strang and G. Stimson (eds.) *Aids and Drug Misuse: The Challenge for Policy and Practice in the 1990s*. London: Routledge.

Casey, M., Day, S., Ward, H., Ziersch, A. (1995) *Sexual Health Services for Prostitutes in the UK*. London: EUROPAP UK.

Centrepoint (1995) Statistics: April 1994 to March 1995. London: Centrepoint.

Centres for Disease Control (1991) *HIV/AIDS Surveillance Report*, September.

Centres for Disease Control (1993) *HIV/AIDS Surveillance Report*, third quarter edition, October.

Children's Legal Centre (1992) *Working with Young People: Legal Responsibility and Liability*. Colchester: Children's Legal Centre.

Children's Legal Centre (1996a) 'Black youth homelessness – a serious problem?' *Childright*, no. 124, p. 5.

Children's Legal Centre (1996b) 'Youth homelessness: A new guide to the provision of services'. *Childright*, no. 127, p. 13.

Cliffe, D. (1990) 'Warwickshire's minefield'. *Community Care*, no. 837, 25 October, p. 8.

Cockrell, J., Hoffman, D. (1989) 'Identifying the needs of boys at risk in prostitution'. *Social Work Today*, vol. 20, no. 36, pp. 20–1.

Coleman, R., Curtis, D., Sharpe, M. (1989) 'The role of the satellite clinic in reaching intravenous drug users at risk from HIV'. *Psychiatric Bulletin*, vol. 13, pp. 165–8.

Council of Europe (1993) *Sexual Exploitation, Pornography and Prostitution of, and Trafficking in, Children and Young Adults*. Strasbourg: Council of Europe.

Council of Europe (1994) *Street Children*. Strasbourg: Council of Europe.

Crimmens, D. (1991) 'Running out of care'. J. Dennington and J. Pitts (eds.) *Developing Services for Young People in Crisis*. Harlow: Longman.

Cunnington, S. (1980) 'Some aspects of prostitution in the west of London'. D. J. West (ed.) *Sex Offenders in the Criminal Justice System*. Cropwood Conference, Series 12. Institute of Criminology, University of Cambridge.

Currie, E. (1991) 'International developments in crime and social policy'. *NACRO Crime and Public Policy*. London: NACRO.

Datt, N., Feinmann, C. (1990) 'Providing health care for drug users?'. *British Journal of Addiction*, vol. 85, no. 12, pp. 1571–6.

Davies, N. (1994) 'Children of the night'. *The Guardian*, 29 August.

Davies, J., Lyle, S. *et al.* (1996) *Discounted Voices: Homelessness amongst Young Black and Minority Ethnic People in England*. University of Leeds.

Davis, M. (1990) *City of Quartz*. London: Verso Ltd.

Dean, H. (1995) 'Family debts, biological liabilities'. H. Dean (ed.) *Parents' Duties, Children's Debts*. Aldershot: Arena Press.

Delors, J. (1993) *Growth, Competitiveness, Employment: The Challenges and Ways Forward into the 21st Century*. Brussels: Commission of the European Communities.

Department for Education and Employment (1995) *Protecting Children from Abuse: The Role of the Education Service*. Circular number 10/95. London: The DfEE Publications Centre.

Department of Health (1989) *An Introduction to the Children Act: A New Framework for the Care and Upbringing of Children*. London: HMSO.

Department of Health (1991) *The Health of the Nation: A Consultative Document for Health in England*. London: HMSO.

Department of Health (1995) *Child Protection: Messages from Research*. London: HMSO.

Department of Health (1996a) *Report of the Task Force to Review Services for Drug Misusers: An Independent Review of Drug Treatment Services in England*. London: Department of Health.

Department of Health (1996b) *Focus on Teenagers: Research into Practice*. London: HMSO.

Department of Health, Home Office, Department of Education and Science and Welsh Office (1991) *Working Together Under the Children Act 1989: A Guide to Arrangements for Inter-agency Co-operation for the Protection of Children from Abuse.* London: HMSO.

Department of Social Security (1995) Households Below Average Income Statistics. London: HMSO.

Des Jarlais, D., Friedman, S. (1987) 'Editorial review: HIV infection among intravenous drug users: Epidemiology and risk reduction'. *AIDS*, vol. 1, issue i, pp. 67–76.

Dibblin, J. (1991) *Wherever I Lay my Hat: Young Women and Homelessness.* London: Shelter – The National Campaign for Homeless People.

Donoghoe, M., Stimson, G., Dolan K. (1989) 'Sexual behaviour of injecting drug users and associated risks of HIV infection for non-injecting sexual partners'. *AIDS Care*, no. 1, pp. 51–58.

Donovan, K. (1991) *Hidden from View: An Exploration of the Little Known World of Young Male Prostitutes in Great Britain and Europe.* London and Birmingham: Home Office and West Midlands Police.

Easton, L. (1996) 'House hunting'. *Community Care*, no. 119, 9–15 May, pp.18–9.

Elion, R. (1990) 'Primary care: The challenge of HIV infection to the care of the drug taker'. J. Strang and G. V. Stimson (eds.) *AIDS and Drug Misuse: The Challenge for Policy and Practice in the 1990s.* London: Routledge.

English Collective of Prostitutes (1996) Information pack.

English Collective of Prostitutes (1997) 'Campaigning for legal change'. G. Scrambler and A. Scrambler (eds.) *Rethinking Prostitution: Purchasing Sex in the 1990s.* London: Routledge.

Ennew, J. (1986) *The Sexual Exploitation of Children.* Cambridge Polity Press.

Ennew, J. (1994) *Street and Working Children: A Guide to Planning.* London: Save the Children Fund.

Essen, J., Lambert, L., Head, J. (1976) 'School attainment of children who have been in care'. *Child: Care, Health and Development*, vol. 2, pp. 339–351.

Ettorre, E. (1992) *Women and Substance Use.* New Brunswick, New Jersey: Rutgers University Press.

Faugier, J. (1996) 'Looking for business: A descriptive study of drug using female prostitutes, their clients and their health care needs'. Ph.D. Thesis, Manchester University.

Finklehor, D. (1986) *A Sourcebook on Child Sexual Abuse.* London: Sage Publications.

Foster, C. (1991) *Male Youth Prostitution.* Norwich: University of East Anglia, Social Work Monographs.

The Guardian (22 August, 1996) I. S. Mawson, co-ordinator, St Hilda's Education Project, Middlesbrough. Letters, p. 18.

German Ministry for the Family (Bundesministerium fur Familie, Senioren, Frauen und Jugend) (1994) 'The future of the family in Europe: The family in Europe at the close of the 20th century'. 13–14 September, Bonn: Documentation.

Gibson, B. (1995) *Male Order*. London: Cassell plc.

Goldstein, P. J. (1979) *Prostitution and Drugs*. New York: Lexington Books.

Gossop, M., Powis, B., Griffiths, P., Strang, J. (1994) 'Sexual behaviour and its relationship to drug-taking among prostitutes in south London'. *Addiction*, vol. 89, no. 8, pp. 961–70.

Gostick, C. (1991) 'Managing change and improving services for young people in crisis'. J. Dennington and J. Pitts (eds.) *Developing Services for Young People in Crisis*. Harlow: Longman.

Graham, J., Bowling, B. (1995) *Young People and Crime*. London: Home Office.

Green, J. (1992) *It's No Game*. Leicester: National Youth Agency.

Hall, R. for Women Against Rape (1985) *Ask Any Woman: A London Inquiry into Rape and Sexual Assault*. London: Falling Wall Press.

Hanslope, J., Waite, M. (1994) 'Safer on the streets'. *Health Lines*, vol. 10, pp. 20–1.

Health Visitors Association (1994) *A Cause for Concern: An Analysis of Staffing Levels and Training Plans in Health Visiting and School Nursing*. London: Health Visitors Association.

Heinz, K. (1992) 'Adolescents at risk from HIV infection'. R. J. DiClemente (ed.) *Adolescents and AIDS*. Newbury Park, C.A: Sage Publications.

Henderson, S. (unpublished 1992) 'Time for a make-over? Gender and drugs today'. Manchester: Drug Resource Unit.

Hendessi, M. (1992) *4 in 10: Report on Young Women who Become Homeless as a Result of Sexual Abuse*. London: CHAR.

Holmes, R. (1995) Dissertation for the Metropolitan Police Clubs and Vice Unit handling of kerb crawling, loitering and soliciting in Marylebone and Bow Street Magistrates' Courts in 1995.

Home Office (1996) *Action against the Commercial Sexual Exploitation of Children*. London: Home Office.

Hope, T. (1994) 'Communities, crime and inequality in England and Wales'. Paper presented to the Cropwood Round Table Conference, Preventing Crime and Disorder, 14–16 September.

International Catholic Child Bureau (1987) 'A universal phenomenon'. *Children Worldwide*, vol. 14, no. 3, pp. 8–18.

Jackson, S. (unpublished 1983) 'The education of children in care: A position paper for the SSRC, Child Care Panel'. University of Bristol, School of Applied Social Studies.

Jaget, C. (ed.) (1980) *Prostitutes: Our Life*. London: Falling Wall Press.

James, S. (1983) 'Hookers in the House of the Lord'. J. Holland (ed.) *Feminist Action*. London: Battle Axe Books.

Jesson, J. (1991) *Young Women in Care: The Social Services Care System and Juvenile Prostitution*. Birmingham City Council, Social Services Department.

Jesson, J., Luck, M., Taylor, J. (1991) *Women and HIV*. Research report for West Birmingham Health Authority. West Birmingham Health Authority Health Promotion Unit.

Jesson, J. (1993) 'Understanding adolescent female prostitution: A literature review'. *British Journal of Social Work*, vol. 23, no. 5, pp. 517–30.

Joseph, C. (1995) 'Scarlet wounding: Issues of child prostitution'. *Journal of Psychohistory*, vol. 23, no. 1, pp. 2–17.

Joseph Rowntree Foundation (1996) *The Future of Work: Contributions to the Debate*. York: Joseph Rowntree Foundation.

Kahan, B. (1985) *Growing up in Care*. Oxford: Basil Blackwell Ltd.

Kelly, L., Scott, S. (1993) 'The current literature about organised abuse of children'. *Child Abuse Review*, vol. 2, no. 4, pp. 281–7.

Kelly, L., Wingfield, R., Burton, S., Regan, L. (1995) *Splintered Lives: Sexual Exploitation of Children in the Context of Children's Rights and Child Protection*. London: Barnardo's.

Kinnell, H. (1991) *Prostitutes' Experiences of Being in Care: Results of a Safe Project Investigation*. Birmingham Community Health Trust, Safe Project.

Kinnell, H. (unpublished 1992) 'SAFE: HIV prevention project'. Collection of papers.

Kinnell, H. (1993) 'Prostitutes exposure to rape: Implications for HIV prevention and for legal reform'. Paper presented to the Seventh Social Aspects of AIDS Conference, June.

Kirby, P. (1995) *A Word from the Street: Young People who Leave Care and Become Homeless*. London: Centrepoint/Community Care/Reed Business Publishing.

Klee, H., Faugier, J., Hayes, C. (1990a) 'Factors associated with risk behaviour among injecting drug users'. *AIDS Care*, no. 2, pp. 133–54.

Klee, H., Faugier, J., Hayes, C. (1990b) 'Sexual partners of injecting drug users: The risk of HIV infection'. *British Journal of Addiction*, vol. 85, no. 3, pp. 413–8.

Klee, H., Lewis, S., Jackson, M. (unpublished 1995) 'Illicit drug use, pregnancy and early motherhood: An analysis of the impediments to effective service delivery'. A report prepared for the Department of Health.

Klein, H., Pittman, D. J. (1993) 'The relationship between emotional state and alcohol consumption'. *International Journal of the Addictions*, vol. 28, pp. 47–61.

Kroll, B., Barrett, D. (1995) 'Troublesome children: Failure and moral liability'. H. Dean (ed.) *Parents' Duties, Children's Debts*. Aldershot: Arena Press.

Kufeldt, K. (1991) 'Social policy and runaways'. *Journal of Health and Social Policy*, vol. 2, no. 4, pp. 37–49.

Lee, M., O'Brien, R. (1995) *The Game's Up: Redefining Child Prostitution*. London: The Children's Society.

Legal Action for Women, Women Against Rape (1995) *Dossier: The Crown Prosecution Service and the Crime of Rape*. London: Crossroads Books.

Londsdale, S. (1994) 'Unfair play on the game'. *The Independent*, 31 July.

Maher, P. (1987) *Child Abuse: The Educational Perspective*. Oxford: Basil Blackwell Ltd.

Mandelson, P., Liddle, R. (1996) *The Blair Revolution: Can New Labour Deliver?*. London: Faber.

Marchant, C. (1993) 'At Risk'. *Community Care*, no. 986, 30 September, pp. 18–9.

Marsh, J. C., Miller, N. A. (1985) 'Female clients in substance abuse treatment'. *International Journal of the Addictions*, vol. 20, pp. 995–1019.

Masterson, A. (1995) 'Why nurses need to know about social policy'. *Surgical Nurse*, no. 8: 2, April, pp. 4–6.

Matthews, R. (1986) 'Beyond Wolfenden?: Prostitution, politics and the law'. R. Matthews and J. Young (eds.) *Confronting Crime*. London: Sage Publications.

Matza, D. (1964) *Delinquency and Drift*. New York: John Wiley.

McCarthy, B., Hagan, J. (1992) 'Surviving on the street: The experience of homeless youth'. *Journal of Adolescent Research*, vol. 7, no. 4, pp. 412–30.

McCormack, M., Janus, D., Burgess, A. (1986) 'Runaway youths and sexual victimisation: Gender differences in an adolescent runaway population'. *Child Abuse and Neglect*, vol. 10, no. 3, pp. 387–95.

McGahey, R. M. (1986) 'Economic conditions, neighbourhood organisation and urban crime'. A. J. Reiss and M. Tonry (eds.) *Communities and Crime*. University of Chicago Press.

McKeganey, N., Barnard, M., Bloor, M., Leyland, A. (1990) 'Injecting, drug use and female street-working in Glasgow'. *AIDS*, vol. 1, issue ii, pp. 1153–5.

McKeganey, M., Barnard, M., Leyland, A. (1993) 'Risk behaviours among male clients of female prostitutes'. *British Medical Journal*, vol. 307, pp. 361–2.

McMullen, R. (1987) 'Youth prostitution: A balance of power'. *Journal of Adolescence*, vol. 10, no. 1, pp. 35–43.

Messerschmidt, J. W. (1993) *Masculinity and Crime: Critique and Reconceptualisation of Theory*. Maryland: Rowman & Littlefield.

Miller, J. (1995) 'Gender and power on the streets: Street prostitution in the era of crack cocaine'. *Journal of Contemporary Ethnography*, vol. 23, pp. 427–52.

Mills, C. W. (1957) *The Sociological Imagination*. Harmondsworth: Penguin Books Ltd.

Milne, R., Keen, S. (1988) 'Are general practitioners ready to prevent the spread of HIV?'. *British Medical Journal*, vol. 296, pp. 533–5.

Morgan Thomas, R., Plant, M. A., Plant, M. L., Sales, J. (1990) 'Risk of infection among clients of the sex industry in Scotland'. *British Medical Journal*, vol. 301, p. 525.

Moss, M., Sharpe, S., Fay, C. (1990) *Abuse in the Care System: A Pilot Study by the National Association of Young People in Care*. Manchester: National Association of Young People in Care.

Mulroy, S., O'Neill, M. (unpublished 1997) 'Comparative analysis of prostitution in England and Spain'. Report for the British Council.

Nelson-Zlupko, L., Morrison Dore, M., Kauffman, E., Kaltenbach, K. (1995) 'Women in recovery: Their perceptions of treatment effectiveness'. *Journal of Substance Misuse*, vol. 13, no. 1, pp. 51–9.

Neville, N. G., McKelligan, J. F., Foster, J. (1988) 'Heroin users in general practice: Ascertainment and features'. *British Medical Journal*, vol. 296, pp. 755–8.

Newman, C. (1989) *Young Runaways: Findings from Britain's First Safe House*. London: The Children's Society.

NHS Health Advisory Service (1996) *Children and Young People: Substance Misuse Services – the Substance of Young Needs*. London: HMSO.

Nicholsen, A. H. (1981) *Youth in Crisis: A Study of Adolescent and Child Prostitution*. Los Angeles: California Gay and Lesbian Community Services Centre.

Observer (24 July, 1994) Karen Bibby, Birmingham. Letters, p. 24.

O'Neill, M. (1996) *Young People in Care: Feminising Theory/ Theorising Sex*. No. 5, Monograph Series, March. Housing and Community Research Unit, Staffordshire University.

O'Neill, M., Goode, N., Hopkins, K. *et al.* (1995) 'Juvenile prostitution: The experience of young women in residential care'. *Childright*, no. 113, pp. 14–6.

Patel, G. (1994) *The Porth Project: A Study of Homelessness and Running Away Amongst Vulnerable Black People in Newport, Gwent*. London: The Children's Society.

Pearson, G. (1987) *The New Heroin Users*. Oxford: Basil Blackwell Ltd.

Pitts, J. (1991) 'Less harm or more good?: Politics, research and practice with young people in crisis'. J. Dennington and J. Pitts (eds.) *Developing Services for Young People in Crisis*. Harlow: Longman.

Pitts, M. (1992) 'Somewhere to run'. BA Dissertation, University of Exeter.

Pitts, J. (1995) 'Public issues and private troubles: A tale of two cities'. *Social Work in Europe*, vol. 2, no. 1, pp. 3–11.

Plant, M. A., Foster, J. (1991) 'Teenagers and alcohol: Results of a Scottish national survey'. *Drug and Alcohol Dependence*, vol. 28, pp. 203–10.

Pritchard, C. (1995) *Suicide – the Ultimate Rejection?: A Psycho-social Study*. Buckingham: Open University Press.

Rees, G. (1993) *Hidden Truths: Young People's Experiences of Running Away*. London: The Children's Society.

Robinson, K. (1995) 'Reviewing the literature'. *Surgical Nurse*, no. 8: 2, April, pp. 7–9.

Rotheram-Borus, M. J., Koopman, C. (1991) 'Sexual risk behaviours: AIDS knowledge and beliefs about AIDS among runaways'. *American Journal of Public Health*, vol. 81, pp. 208–210.

Russell, D. (1986) *The Secret Trauma*. New York: Basic Books.

Sadler, C. (1994) 'Child protection: Is working together falling apart?'. *Health Visitor*, vol. 67, no. 8, pp. 259–60.

Segal, L. (1990) *Slow Motion: Changing Masculinities, Changing Men*. London: Virago Press.

Segal, V., Schwartz, S. (1987) 'Admission-discharge patterns in children in emergency treatment shelters: Implications for child and youth care practitioners'. *Child and Youth Care Quarterly*, vol. 16, no. 4, Winter, pp. 263–71.

The San Francisco Task Force on Prostitution (1996) *Final Report*. City and County of San Francisco, California.

Seng, M. (1989) 'Child sexual abuse and adolescent prostitution: A comparative analysis, *Adolescence*, vol. 24, no. 95, pp. 665–75.

Sereny, G. (1984) *The Invisible Children: Child Prostitution in America, Germany and Britain*. London: Deutsch.

Sheridan, M. J. (1995) 'A proposed intergenerational model of substance abuse, family functioning and abuse/neglect'. *Child Abuse and Neglect*, vol. 19, no. 5, pp. 519–30.

Shriane, H. (1995) *Luton Runaways Profile*. Luton Community Links Project.

Silbert, M., Pines, A. (1981) 'Sexual child abuse as an antecedent to prostitution'. *Child Abuse and Neglect*, vol. 5, pp. 407–11.

Silverman, A., Reinherz, H., Giaconia, R. (1996) 'The long-term sequelae of child and adolescent abuse: A longitudinal community study'. *Child Abuse and Neglect*, vol. 20, no. 8, pp. 709–23.

Shaw, I., Butler, I., Crowley, A. with Patel, G. (1996) *Paying the Price: Young People and Prostitution in South Glamorgan*. School of Social and Administrative Studies, University of Wales College of Cardiff.

Shaw, I., Butler, I. (forthcoming 1998) 'Research into young people and prostitution: A foundation for practice?'. *British Journal of Social Work*, February.

Sibley, D. (1995) *Geographies of Exclusion*. London: Routledge.

Slonim-Nevo, V., Auslander, W., Ozawa, M., Jung K. (1996) 'The long-term impact of AIDS-preventative interventions for delinquent and abused adolescents'. *Adolescence*, vol. 31, no. 122, pp. 409–21.

Stein, M., Frost, N., Rees, G. (1994) *Running the Risk: Young People on the Streets of Britain Today*. London: The Children's Society.

Stiffman, A., Earls, F., Robins, L., Jung, K. (1988) 'Problems and help-seeking in high-risk adolescents'. *Journal of Adolescent Health Care*, vol. 9, July, pp. 305–9.

Swingler, N. (1969) 'The streetwalker's return'. *New Society*, 16 January, pp. 81–3.

Sykes, G., Matza, D. (1957) 'Techniques of neutralisation: A theory of delinquency'. *American Sociological Review*, vol. 22, pp. 664–70.

Taylor, S., Tilley, N. (1989) 'Health visitors and child protection: Conflict, contradictions and ethical dilemmas'. *Health Visitor*, vol. 62, no. 9, pp. 273–5.

Thomson, A. (1989) 'Crisis on the street'. *Community Outlook*, January, pp. 8–9.

Van der Ploeg, J. (1989) 'Homelessness: A multi-dimensional problem'. *Children and Youth Services Review*, vol. 11, no. 1, pp. 45–62.

Warburton, J., Camacho de la Cruz, M. (1996) 'A right to happiness: Approaches to the prevention and psycho-social recovery of child victims of commercial sexual exploitation'. Paper submitted by Barnardo's to the World Congress against Commercial Sexual Exploitation of Children, Stockholm. Chelmsford: UNICEF/ECPAT.

Watt, G. (1996) 'A place for children in Europe'. *Childright*, no. 123, pp. 12–13.

Weisberg, D. K. (1985) *Children of the Night: A Study of Adolescent Prostitution*. Massachusetts: Lexington Books.

Wells, M., Berridge, D. (1995) *Social Indicators and Recorded Crime in Luton*. University of Luton Centre for the Study of Crime and Urban Regeneration.

West, A. (1988) 'Reducing the options'. *Youth in Society*, no. 145, December.

West, D., De Villiers, B. (1992) *Male Prostitution: Gay Sex Services in London*. London: Duckworth.

White, D., Phillips, K., Mulleady, G., Cupitt, C. (1993) 'Sexual issues and condom use among injecting drug users'. *AIDS Care*, vol. 5, no. 4, pp. 427–37.

Widom, C. S., Ames, M. A. (1994) 'Criminal consequences of childhood sexual victimisation'. *Child Abuse and Neglect*, vol. 18, no. 4, pp. 303–18.

Women Against Rape (1996) Information pack.

Women Against Rape (forthcoming) 'Suffer the little children'. *The Right to Refuse: Rape in the Home and Outside*. London: Crossroads Books.

Yates, G., MacKenzie, R., Pennbridge, J., Cohen, J. (1988) 'A risk profile comparison of runaway and non-runaway youth'. *American Journal of Public Health*, vol. 78, no. 7, pp. 820–1.

Yates, G., MacKenzie, R., Pennbridge, J., Swofford, A. (1991) 'A risk profile comparison of homeless youth involved in prostitution and homeless youth not involved'. Special issue: homeless youth. *Journal of Adolescent Health*, vol. 12, no. 7, pp. 545–8.

Index

THE CHILDREN'S SOCIETY

The Children's Society is a Christian organisation which exists to work with and for children and young people, regardless of race, culture or creed.

The Children's Society runs more than 90 projects throughout England and Wales, including:

- family centres and neighbourhood groups in local communities where families are under stress, often feeling isolated and powerless to improve their lives;

- providing independent living units for young people leaving care;

- working with young people living on the street;

- offering independent guardians *ad litem* for children involved in care proceedings;

- residential and day care for children and young people with disabilities;

- helping children and young people with special needs to find new families;

- promoting the rights of children and young people.

The Children's Society is committed to raising public awareness of issues affecting children and young people and to promoting their welfare and rights in matters of public policy. The Society produces a wide range of publications, including reports, briefing papers and educational material.

For further information about the work of The Children's Society or to obtain a publications list, please contact:

The Publications Department
The Children's Society
Edward Rudolf House
Margery Street
London WC1X 0JL

Tel. 0171-837 4299
Fax 0171-837 0211